ADVENTURES OF A YOUNG MARINE IN WW II

A memoir of an impressionable teenager's
tour of duty of four wartime years
in the U.S. Marine Corps,
including eighteen months in the
South-Central Pacific theater

by

WALT "KELLY" AUGUSTYNIAK

USMC

September 1941 – November 1945

Produced and published by Walter Augustyniak
Printed in the United States of America

Library of Congress Control Number: 2017915920

ISBN-13: 978-0-692-96089-9 (pbk)

DEDICATION

This book is dedicated to the many Marines in WW II who served overseas, but received little or no acknowledgement or glory for their hard work and dedication. Even though they were able to live in a mostly clean environment, never having to suffer the stress of combat, or ever having to spend a night in a foxhole, their lonely life in these distant lands was far from being a bed of roses. It is no less dedicated to my ever patient and faithful high school sweetheart, Neshie, who waited four long years for my return from the Marines, and who then provided me with 66 years of blissful marriage and three loving children.

ADVENTURES
OF A
YOUNG MARINE
IN WW II

The Author on weekend leave, 1942

ACKNOWLEDGEMENTS

This book was originally intended for my close family, but after discovering my probing memory so able to bring back to life so many personal experiences, I became convinced it should be made available to the general public. While overseas during this period of time, we servicemen were under strict rules of censorship: no cameras and no diaries were allowed, and all outgoing mail was strictly censored. In addition to relying heavily on recalling distant memories, I needed the statistics found in my records obtained from The National Archives, details from my Aviator's Flight Log Book, and also data from today's very informative Internet. I am thankful to my grandson, Bill Brittelle, who was the first to convince me to start getting my oft told "war stories" down on paper, for my family members who kept coaxing me to get it done, and for the initial editing put forth by a good friend, Mary Lawler. But most of all, many thanks to my son, Michael, who put in countless hours in the editing of this book and getting it entered into the mills of publication.

FOREWORD

This book attempts to portray the life of a very young Marine while he dutifully served his country during the era immediately preceding December 7th and throughout the entire WW-II years that followed. He never participated in any combat, but did spend 18 months overseas in the South-Central Pacific, in support of combat operations in that theater.

Many fascinating books have already been written by combat veterans, or by their biographers. However, this story may be one of few to attempt a description of what life was like for the average Marine stationed behind battle lines,... one who never did taste combat. The author recalls and gives vivid accounts of the many good and bad adventures he experienced during his tour of duty as a US Marine.

TABLE OF CONTENTS

PART 1 - ENLISTMENT, BOOT CAMP, AND SCHOOL 1
1. ON THE WAY 1
2. PARRIS ISLAND...4
3. THE RIFLE RANGE 13
4. QUANTICO - AVIATION ORDNANCE SCHOOL................20
5. DAHLGREN, VA - NAVY BOMBSIGHT SCHOOL.............29
6. THE CLASSROOM 35

PART 2 - HEADING WEST, AND TO THE PACIFIC......................44
7. WITH NEW RECRUITS ON A CROSS COUNTRY TRAIN....44
8. SAN DIEGO NAVAL AIR STATION................................49
9. LONG JOURNEY ACROSS THE PACIFIC 60

PART 3 – OVERSEAS: SAMOA, AND ON TO TARAWA.............68
10. SETTLING IN..68
11. ASSUMING DUTIES 83
12. THE TRAGIC CELEBRATION 91
13. A NEW TROPICAL DISEASE..95
14. PREPARING FOR THE BIG PUSH 98
15. WORKING ON PBYs – A TRIP TO AUSTRALIA? 100
16. MY NEW QUARTERS...104
17. TAKING TARAWA, THE GILBERTS & THE MARSHALLS 113
18. FLIGHT TO TARAWA WITH GENERAL PRICE 120
19. TRIP TO FIJI...127
20. ABOARD A RESCUE MISSION 132
21. BRIEF PARADISE ON A TROPICAL ISLE 140
22. THE VOYAGE HOME 146

PART 4 - FURLOUGHS, FLYING AND FUN 151
23. THE LONG AWAITED 30 DAY FURLOUGH.....................151
24. MCAS, SANTA BARBARA..160
25. MCAS, EL CENTRO, AND THE DESERT 164
26. BOMBARDIER SCHOOL...166
27. LIVING IT UP...180
28. HEADING HOME 183

EPILOGUE..186
29. KEEPING IN TOUCH WITH OLD COMRADES....................186

ITINERARY 190

POST-WAR ACTIVITIES...191

PART 1 - ENLISTMENT, BOOT CAMP, AND SCHOOL

1. ON THE WAY

It was the summer of 1941. The place was a small coal mining town in Northeastern Pennsylvania. Only 16 years old, I had just graduated from Ashley High School and had no plans for the future. There were no other opportunities in the area other than working as a coal miner, a dirty and most dangerous job. I graduated as valedictorian of my class, but could not afford the expenses of a college education, and there were no scholarships awarded in those days. In fact, my high school did not even issue special certificates to the top graduating students. There happened to be a branch junior college in the nearby city of Wilkes-Barre, but my family could not afford to send me there. My high school offered no encouragement in pursuit of a higher education. Up to now, I had worked only as an office cleaner, a paper boy, and a painter's apprentice.

However, with the escalation of world hostilities, the US government opened up a limited educational opportunity to recent high school graduates by offering a free ten week credited course in Accelerated Engineering. It was a summer course, offered in the vacant summer classrooms of the Bucknell Junior College in Wilkes-Barre, supervised by Pennsylvania State College, and taught by professors hired from outlying universities. I jumped at the opportunity.

I attended all-day classes in the heart of the city, and spent lunch hours relaxing in the public square, in the city's center. I soon discovered that not far from that location was the local US Marine recruiting office. And there I soon spent many noon hours chatting with the recruiting sargent. As a growing teenager, I was somewhat infatuated in learning about the many brave deeds by the US Marines. The local movie house presented many exciting Saturday afternoon serials, such as the Lone Ranger. One of these serials especially caught my interest. It was called "The Fighting US Devildogs," an older name given to the Marines. These heroes did not fight wars in foreign countries, but displayed their courage in chasing domestic bad guys, like smugglers, pirates and such. So, gradually, my visits to the recruiting office took on a more serious tone. The Sarge soon became my confidant. The office itself was a very pleasant room, with dark, freshly varnished walls, and a very high ceiling. It had an almost euphoric aroma of old wood and varnish about it, and I found it to be a pleasure just to lounge in. I felt at home in this office. The Sarge had a nice way about him, and one found it easy to discuss a few very difficult subjects with him, like the most embarrassing of all: the sexual problems of a teenage boy. My parents were from the old country, and discussing sex with their children was completely out of the question. So, by the end of the summer without realizing it, I was slowly being drawn into the ranks of the famed United States Marine Corps.

The Sarge had me examined by a local doctor and dentist. I looked okay to qualify on the medical front, but failed when it came to teeth. I was the youngest of eight children, and none of us had ever owned a toothbrush. In the old country, sugar and other sweets were scarcities, so the population suffered very few cavities. At age 72, my father still had his original teeth. But here in the USA, it was a different story, with candy in abundance. So, I first had to get my teeth fixed before I could be allowed to sign up with the Marines. It was a tough sell to get my mother to advance me the money to have this done. For most of the summer, I spent three days a week in the local dentist's chair having a total of 21 cavities filled. All my molars required extensive drilling. There were no local anesthetics given to dental patients in those days. You simply had to endure the pain. You might say that this sort of helped prepare me for any pains that might come about while getting groomed in boot camp. So, after successfully completing the course in Engineering, having my teeth fixed to meet the minimum requirements, and getting my parents written consent for enlisting under the age of eighteen, the papers were then prepared for me to sign up for a four year tour of duty with the Marines. I would not be 17 until the day I was to depart for the Philadelphia Recruiting Station for a full physical, swearing in, and transport to boot camp in South Carolina. The Sarge was delighted to also garnish another desirable recruit, an all American football player from Kingston, a large suburb of Wilkes-Barre. This bit of news was submitted to the official Marine Corps magazine, the Leatherneck, which announced, "This day, the Marine Corps benefited both intellectually and athletically with the enlistment of so and so."

I was surprised to learn that in a typical recruiting year, the Wilkes-Barre - Scranton area sent more recruits to Parris Island, SC, than did the New York City area. This was an indicator of the poor work opportunities that existed in the coal region, and perhaps the prevailing motive for enlistments; that being the desire for three square meals a day and having a warm place to sleep. It seemed that I would no longer need to worry about finding suitable local employment. I would have to leave behind Neshie, my high school sweetheart, but there's an old saying "absence makes the heart grow fonder." We were neighbors and had become totally committed to each other, a genuine case of teenage puppy love. Our relationship was starting to get serious, but because of our tender age and lack of employment opportunities, we felt that my going away for four years would be a true test of our devotion to each other. Also, I did possess a strong sense of patriotism, and felt that becoming a serviceman in this time of world strife would be the right thing to do. The latter was the basic argument I used to convince my parents to sign the required consent form.

On the morning of my 17th birthday, September 22, 1941, I found myself at the spacious Philadelphia Marine Corps recruiting center. There, a bustle of activity abounded as additional recruits from nearby areas were arriving. We all had our pictures taken, each wearing the famous Marine Blues uniform, which had been borrowed from Marine office workers. My photo showed a beaming young lad, but little did I know that I would never again wear or own a set of these sharp looking Blues. They were issued to very few types of Marines; only those who served in recruiting offices, aboard ships, embassies and government official guards, etc. Other Marines were allowed to buy these colorful uniforms, but very few did since they were costly and well beyond our means, as our starting pay was a mere $21 per month. So, it would only be khakis and forest greens for the average Marine.

Swearing in at Philadelphia   Six days later in Boot Camp

2. PARRIS ISLAND

With an accompanying escort, our group of recruits traveled by train to Yemassee, SC. Along the way, we picked up a few more candidates. After disembarking from the train, we assembled for a customary roll call, followed by a bus ride to Parris Island. The attending Sargent first rendered a few unflattering comments about "This sad looking bunch of misfits," and then started to make his way down our alphabetical list of names. In trying to read my name out loud, he began stuttering when half way through my last name of Augustyniak. He then wisely switched to spelling it, but soon realized that too was going to be a chore. So, without further hesitation, he barked... "KELLY!" I got the message, and immediately responded: "HERE!" This new name stuck with me for most of my tour in the Corps. To this day, when I hear someone yell "KELLY," I automatically respond.

We didn't get into any kind of training for a few days. The reason was simple... this was still peacetime, and even though Parris Island was the boot camp for the entire eastern half of the USA, the typical daily number of recruits drifting into camp was meager. So, it took over a week to accumulate enough men to form a double platoon (about 124 men). In the meantime, the days were busy with issuance of uniforms, medical shots, and in general, lots of lectures. Finally, we were all set. I was assigned to Platoon 148. To this day, this number has something magic about it. Each and every day, we were instilled with pride and inspiration that we were to strive to be the best platoon the Corps ever pushed through boot camp.

Our NCO was Gunnery Sgt. Harrison. He was a career Marine, and originally from South Carolina. From our first lecture, we were all inspired with this leader, and I'm sure everyone else felt as I did about wanting to have him as our leader in any future, grave situation. Since this was 1941, there were very few active Marines possessing combat experience from global wars, such as the 1914-1918 World War I. However, in Nicaragua in 1928, during a period of political instability, Sgt. Harrison, with the Marines, had spent many months chasing down Sandinista rebels. We loved hearing him relate his exciting stories about surviving some tense situations he had experienced. Many of these inspiring lectures focused on how we young recruits could aspire to become outstanding Marines.

On the other hand, every platoon had assigned to it a drill instructor. Yes, the infamous "DI". And our platoon did unfortunately draw one of the meanest and uncivilized DIs of all time. His name was Corporal Huey, a native of Brooklyn, NY. He was cold and merciless. We often wondered how our affable Sargent, to whom Huey had to report, tolerated some of the inhumane acts that we were forced to endure. However, this treatment is often portrayed as being essential in the making of a man out of a raw recruit. The Sarge probably knew all along what was going on, and had his finger on the HALT button on more than one occasion, but knew we needed this caliber of rough training. Early on, most of us must have had reservations as to whether we could finish boot camp successfully, as it really took more than stamina. Above all, you had to have determination, the deep desire to do good in all things. Then with pride, you could call yourself a Marine. Without let up, you were put to the test each and every day.

I found that physical strength need not be the major factor for survival. I had not been endowed with a muscular build and had not played any major sports in high school, although I did always stay physically active. I classified myself as pretty soft when it came to most physical challenges. But here's the clincher. I really didn't have a problem meeting the extreme physical demands imposed on us. I had the determination, right from the first day. I was shy and rather homesick, but I always tried my best. Some of the recruits who were older and also those tougher athletically, may have had a tougher time. The maximum age for recruits was 29 years old, and I noted that anyone over 25 seemed to have more problems, mental as well as physical, than did we teenagers. Of course, it was more natural for youngsters to obey the frequent blind orders dished out to us recruits every day. This age factor seemed to have had a strong psychological influence in achieving a successful finish to boot camp.

A slight feeling of being doomed did occasionally creep over us all. If you physically didn't make it in the first eight week allotted course, you simply had to start boot camp all over again. One recruit who joined our platoon soon after it was formed, was starting his boot camp for the third time. He was a lumberjack from the state of Maine, big and husky, and a real likeable guy. But he just wasn't able to learn how to march, never mastering whether to go left or go right. So, he twice wound up going over the hill, abandoning Parris Island by swimming across a treacherous, shark-infested tidal channel, and making his way across virgin swampland along the coastline. One of his escapes got him all the way to Virginia, but the second one only got him into the nearby swamps, where he was turned in by local natives who were keen in the task of spotting deserters, and were monetarily rewarded for this service. We all felt there should have been an alternate solution to this seemingly eternal boot camp for him. He tried very hard to learn, but it was obvious that he never would, somewhat akin to learning how to dance. Sadly, while attached to our platoon, he went over the hill once more.

Another older recruit named Gibbs, was delighted when called in one day and being informed that, because a check of his background revealed he possessed a felony record, he was to be immediately discharged. When he came into the barracks to pack his belongings and bid us farewell, it was with an air of bravado. "I'm getting out. I'm the lucky one. Tough shit on you poor bastards!" Outwardly, we envied him, but inwardly I'm sure most felt as I did... a little sorry for him. I had a feeling that later in life, he would never publicly brag about this episode.

Another character who caught everyone's eye was Grier, from upstate New York. He was a good looking guy, but his handsome face also sported a beautiful mouse,... in other words, a black eye. While still a civilian, he got into an altercation with someone who happened to have called his sister a whore. Grier assured us that his opponent fared far worse than did he.

Another memorable character, coming straight from the hills of West Virginia, was a real big guy and, as you would have it, bore the spitting image of Li'l Abner of the comic strips. His southern drawl was infectious and did he love to talk. He also found it very difficult to take the continuous abuses from Cpl. Huey. At times, he became so frustrated with Huey, he would insist on having it out with him. Regulations would have none of that, but Li'l Abner kept the challenge alive by proposing to put on the gloves with Huey. Regulations provided for boxing matches among recruits and among DIs, but not between the two groups. Li'l Abner never ceased challenging Huey.

We had a small group of men from the hills of Kentucky and Tennessee who didn't take daily bathing very seriously. This was hard to understand given the new shower facilities we enjoyed. Parris Island is situated very far south, and as such endures much hot and humid weather, even in the fall. The DIs had a solution for guys who refused to shower every day, and that was to see that they received their bath outside... in the parade grounds, using sand instead of soap. The DIs weren't allowed to administer this kind of punishment, but instead, passed it on to the recruits of that particular platoon. And so, the deed was accomplished by our group, and never again needed repeating.

Another character from the Midwest was Benson. Having come from Missouri resulted in his speech to be laden with a very slow, southern drawl. These "foreign" accents were new to me and I enjoyed listening to them. They were almost entertaining. One thing we had to learn fast was how we called ourselves. Of course, we always addressed our platoon Sargent and our DI as "Sir." But as for ourselves, we were Private so and so. One day Cpl. Huey casually approached Benson, asking "What's your name, Private?" The answer came back: "Benson." Whack! Down came Huey's swagger stick across the top of Benson's pith helmet. Huey again barked: "What's your name?" A new answer came back: "Benson, <u>Sir</u>." Whack! Again, Huey: "What's your name?" Now the answer came back: "Private Benson, Sir." He finally got it right. DIs were allowed to carry swagger sticks, but not allowed to use them for corporal punishment. The pith helmet we recruits wore served as an accepted handy target.

As we progressed through our daily paces, there prevailed among us a tremendous degree of pride and achievement. You had to believe your platoon was the very best. We just had to do everything faster and better than all the other platoons going through the same programs. Competition was constantly stressed. The makeup of our platoon was rather diverse. It was my first exposure to Southerners. I wasn't sure I fitted in with them, but I did find one guy, Pierce from Georgia, with whom I immediately bonded. The rest of my pals were mostly New Englanders who made up a big portion of our platoon.

Each boot received the famous ¼ inch crew cut, followed by a volley of inoculations, which amazingly caused a few big of the guys to pass out shortly afterwards while standing at attention. We also listened to a short lecture from the base chaplain. His talk didn't quite fit in with our DI's philosophy. He was elderly and not in uniform, and I got the impression that this was a volunteer job. He had a bad case of palsy, with a marked tremor in one of his hands. The chaplain obviously was encouraged to rush through his sermon in which he managed to stress that we follow our consciences and discard some old Marine Corps philosophies such as you aren't a Marine until you've had a dose of the clap, another word for gonorrhea. Soon after came a visit to the quartermaster for our new clothes.

There, we were to find that one-piece fatigue uniforms were being phased out and we were to be one of the last platoons to be issued that particular style. But the quartermaster had only one size left to issue, and that was LARGE. Since I was 6 foot 2, I had no problems fitting in them. However, the group from Tennessee and Kentucky, who all seemed to be short in stature, barely measured up to the enlistment minimum height of 5 foot 6. So they had to keep their pants legs rolled up in order to navigate, but with their fatigue's crotch halfway down to their knees, marching and running became rather difficult and almost comical to witness. Because of my height, I was assigned as one of the four squad leaders and felt a little sorry for these short guys, all on the tail ends of each squad. I constantly kept trying to slow down the pace, but the DI would respond by barking at me: "STEP OUT, KELLY.... STEP OUT!"

Finally, the day arrived when we were issued what would become our most prized possession, the 1903, 30-06 caliber Springfield rifle. We were most fortunate to be the very first occupants of new, brick faced barracks. Previous platoons had makeshift quarters and many even stayed in tents. We were to enjoy all new conveniences. The brick buildings surrounded a courtyard which gave a soothing, acoustical tone to our daily live bugle calls, especially that of evening Taps. The courtyard also contained the facility for doing our own laundry. This structure consisted of long wooden troughs equipped with running water. A bucket with soap and scrub brush would serve as our laundry appliances. Inside, we took particular pride in the bathrooms, especially the showers. The floors and walls were all tile-lined. The floors were so perfectly smooth that we took pleasure in heavily soaping our buttocks, pushing off one wall and then sliding our sitting bodies across the floors to opposite walls.

One of the heavy hardships thrust upon us that from the day we arrived, was that we were essentially placed under full quarantine. No one was allowed to leave the group even in the off hours. If we wanted to see an evening movie, the entire platoon had to go as one. The same went for religious services. If we were in need of something from the PX (post exchange), one man was designated to take a list of items requested by all individuals, and fulfill them. Phone calls were only occasionally allowed. Most of us couldn't afford the price of a long distance call, anyway. Writing letters to home was our only real contact with the outside world. Visitors were not allowed on the base at any time. There was only one road leading to the base and it was a narrow causeway across the swamp. Even the commanding general would be refused access to the base if he were to forget his ID card. This scenario would make a recruit feel he was in a helpless situation, with no one to turn to. There was no room for cry-babies in boot camp. You're on your own now, Kelly. Do it right and do it fast. That's the only way you'll get out of here.

The very first thing we learned was how to do a platoon formation. All platoons were made up of 72 men, lined up in three double rows of 12 men. At the command of "FALL IN," the men would raggedly assume this formation, then each man would turn his head left and extend his left arm to barely touch the man's shoulder next to him. This provided the proper spacing. The command followed to "COUNT OFF." The first man in each of the four squads would yell out in a gruff voice "ONE" and simultaneously snap his head back to straight forward. Then the second men would likewise yell their number and snap back. However, Platoon 148 had an extra man in our ranks. This made him number thirteen and he stood alone as the last man in one of the four rows. He happened to be a scrawny, hump shouldered, kind of wild eyed kid with a real squeaky voice. To top it off, he happened to be from the Bronx, NY, known for its distinct accent. So, as the count would progress up the numbers scale, each with a chorus of four, deep, manly voices, it would abruptly end with a solitary, squeaky "TOYTEEN." This ritual was always certain to elicit a subdued burst of laughter from all the other boots. Laughing while in ranks was an absolute no-no. However, even our polished and reserved leader, Sgt. Harrison had a tough time stifling his laughter. Eventually, this poor recruit was assigned to the casualty platoon, to be discharged at a later time. These few recruits were mostly mentally challenged in some way, and some just being physically too scrawny. How they ever made it through their respective recruiting station is a mystery. Perhaps it was just to fill an expected quota from that area. These recruits were actually treated as a single, unique platoon, and required to do only menial tasks for about a month until enough money was earned by each for transportation back to their city of origin.

Another character, named Cleary also came from NY. He too was short and not built solid like you would expect to see in a Marine. He sported a pimply face, like he was still in early high school. We felt he would never make it through boot camp and expected him to also wind up in the casualty platoon. However, Cleary did possess an immeasurable amount of determination. We all worked very hard to get through, and Cleary tried even harder. On one occasion, while drilling in the open field, he made the cardinal mistake of referring to his Springfield rifle as his gun. This innocent gaffe would always get the full attention of the DI. Cleary was consequently pulled out of the ranks and made to stand by himself in the middle of the field while holding the rifle in front of him. Then, while loudly reciting "This is my rifle, this is my gun" over and over again, he was then made to shift a hand from the rifle to grab his crotch while continuing with the second half of this litany: "My rifle's for shooting, my gun's for fun." He was forced to keep repeating this litany without end. We must have marched around the field for an hour while Cleary kept up his chant, sometimes fading into hardly being heard, then harshly being reprimanded by Cpl. Huey to keep reciting the litany, and louder. Consequently, we developed a lot of respect for Cleary. Later, we were all happy to learn that after finishing boot camp, he was being assigned to a Balloon Barrage outfit.

The first half of boot camp was devoted to endless sessions of close-order drill and exercise programs, many using the Springfield rifle, which weighed about nine pounds. Sgt. Harrison had promised us in his orientation session that the rigors of boot camp would result in growing muscles in all parts of our bodies. "You shouldn't be surprised to find muscles in your shit," he would say. Meanwhile, Huey was on the drill field, grinding us through the relentless paces of marching as a platoon. I was one of the four designated squad leaders, presumably because of my height. After about a week of intensive marching drills, the latest issue of the Marine Corps magazine, The Leatherneck, happened to hit the stands, and it featured the following article;

> "The Marine Corps today has benefitted both intellectually and athletically with the enlistment at the Wilkes Barre recruiting office of Walt Augustyniak, valedictorian of the 1941 Ashley High School graduating class, and Paul Albosta, an all-American football player, and graduate of Kingston High School."

This article caught Huey's eye. Knowing this, I made extra effort not to screw up. Then, about ten days later, while on the drill field, I made the simple mistake of turning left instead of right. Huey immediately brought the formation to a screeching halt, dashed up to confront me, and shoved his faced just inches from mine. Then with fire in his eyes, he barked, "Intellectually, HA! You're just a stupid shit just like the rest." I could only respond, "Yes Sir!"

Each day, reveille sounded at 4 AM. Before breakfast, the barrack floors had to be scrubbed down by hand, then followed by a command from the DI that we were to hear repeated many times in the oncoming weeks: "FALL OUT!" This simply meant for all to get their butts out of the barracks and line up outside in four ranks as a platoon. But do it with vigor and do it fast! Only, it was never fast enough for Huey, so it had to be repeated over and over. This maneuver sort of set the stage for our DI's upcoming punishing agenda. The open fields of the main camp held endless daily marching and drilling sessions for all the platoons in boot camp. Even when we felt we got those procedures down perfect, they were yet to be repeated many more times. Practice makes perfect sounds like an appropriate motto, but we also did it as a tool to toughen up. We also endured short courses on the proper method of tossing hand grenades, practicing skirmishes with the bayonet, and the very unpleasant experience of exposure to tear gas without a face mask while confined in tiny, unventilated quarters. Finally, we were made to participate in boxing matches, with the combatants being intentionally mismatched.

Soon after, came the long running sessions, eventually progressing with wearing backpacks, and of course, always carrying our rifles. These included endless sessions of "hit the deck" while on a run. The typical boot executed this maneuver rather gently at first. While into a full run, he would, on command and without any hesitation, be required to instantly, and I mean instantly, dive for ground cover. This maneuver required first raising your rifle into a vertical position directly in front of you, going down fast, contacting the ground first with the left knee, then the rifle butt, followed by throwing the rest of your body to the ground. This maneuver doesn't sound too unpleasant, right? What if the ground you were about to hit with gusto wasn't very accommodating? It was taught because, in combat, it might turn out be a life saver, as in the case of a patrol coming under sudden enemy fire. It was to teach you that you didn't have time to search for a nice, cushiony spot to throw yourself down. You had to do it right then and there! To add a little flavor to this tough act, the DIs typically chose a broad field that held a smattering of fallen briers. In hitting the ground there, your elbows and knees became imbedded with a slew of briers, inflicting a somewhat painful experience. After the first try, it was only natural to hesitate just a bit, and try to land a bit gently. So, you had to do it again and again, each time a little faster. In the end, you performed this ritual with enthusiasm, as if you actually enjoyed it. This maneuver might later prove to be a valuable lesson for those having to serve in a combat zone.

3. THE RIFLE RANGE

The day finally came that we all had been anxiously looking forward to: the move to the firing range! Marching and drilling without a token prize in the offering had become rather monotonous routines. But doing something with your rifle looked like fun, and promised to be rewarding. The distance to the rifle range was about eight miles. The first time we ran it was without the backpack. Even though it was exhausting, I especially enjoyed the running, even with the backpack. During these runs, our DI never left our sides, but he carried no rifle or a backpack. At first, it seemed like he had it easy, but in a closer view of performing these runs, I noticed that he kept running almost constantly, up and down the length of two double rows of running recruits as the platoon forged ahead. How could he keep that up? This left no doubt that this guy had to be in great physical shape!

With joyous anticipation, we finally made our move to new quarters at the rifle range, only to first face a real disappointment. These barracks were old wooden buildings and the chow was outright awful. As did many others, I ate very little of the meals there and consequently lost a good bit of weight. At these quarters, reveille now sounded at 3 AM. The wooden barracks floors were old and hard to scrub. We did gain one particular pleasure while in our stay at the rifle range, and that was the temporary absence of Cpl. Huey.

But a second disappointment came our way. We didn't jump directly into using our 30 caliber Springfield rifles. First, we had to spend a few days in practice at the 100 inch firing range, and using much smaller 22 caliber rifles. A distinct lesson was to be learned here, one that the Marine Corps had developed to help mold a Marine into first becoming an excellent rifleman. When fired, the Springfield rendered quite a recoil, so that you felt a decisive kick to your shoulder when the trigger was pulled. A rookie rifleman became very apt to anticipate this kick by throwing his shoulder into the rifle as he squeezed the trigger. This undesirable action was called "bucking" and would send the bullet into the ground, way short of the intended target. This was viewed as a serious obstacle to becoming a good marksman. When fired, the 22 rifle delivered almost no kick, rendering the marksman to readily accept it without bucking.

The 100 inch range spanned a distance of a little over eight feet. Bullseyes were on post card size targets, and held onto a post with a wooden clothespin clip. Since accuracy was not stressed here, the rifle instructors had to find another punishment to bestow upon us. The target card was small and the clothespin clip made it all look rather delicate. Woe to the shooter who hit the clothespin instead of the target. Several recruits did, and as punishment, had to do KP (Kitchen Police) that evening, accompanied by catching a bit of good-natured ribbing from his peers. This course also provided a good outlet for relieving any tensions in the platoon. Evenings were spent learning how to care for your rifle. Disassemble, clean, reassemble. You did this a countless number of times. You learned to do the job while blindfolded. It was imperative you took good care of your "friend," and so it didn't take much coaxing to realize that your rifle was indeed your best friend. One day it might be responsible for saving your life. We all took pride in caring for this friend and welcomed the responsibility.

The 30-06 Springfield was, and remains a precise and powerful weapon, especially at long range. It is equipped with gun sights which allow the operator to set incremental adjustments for distance to the target, as well as to compensate for any cross winds. It is still being used today, but only as a sniper's weapon. It isn't practical in today's combat situations because of its slow, manual bolt-loading action. There was one variation in our weapon carrying agenda. Each platoon had one Marine assigned to carry a BAR, the Browning Automatic Rifle. This weapon carried clips of ammunition which when loaded could produce bursts of 20 rounds without having to reload with the use of bolt action. The BAR did weigh a few pounds more, and was not as accurate at long range, since some of its recoil was used in the automatic reloading process, thus taking away some of the thrust of the exiting bullet.

Firing the 22 was fun (I managed to successfully avoid hitting the clothespin). Shooting accuracy was never stressed. At age 17, I had never held, owned, or operated any sort of firearm. Needless to say, I was somewhat apprehensive when having to mix with the older and experienced shooters, like those in our squad who came from

Kentucky and Tennessee. Now it was on to the real rifle range with our trusty Springfield. That day finally came in late October when we all found ourselves evenly lined up parallel to a neat row of 39 targets far off in the distance. Oh boy, here's where we start having fun and seeing results.

"After you spot your target, keep your eye on it until you get your shot off!"

Recruits on the Firing Line, early 1940s

Note the large number of Firing Instructors; Sargents, wearing the famous broad-billed Campaign hats, and their assistants, all PFCs, wearing plain Garrison caps. It was a necessity to closely mother each and every one of us, since we were now playing with real ammunition. Accidents could easily happen under these circumstances; therefore, we were constantly reminded to always keep our rifle pointed in the direction of the targets. I could still hear the firing instructors shouting off the following commands: "Ready on the right, ready on the left. All ready on the firing line." That called for everyone on the firing line to stay put. Our first shots were from a prone position and consisted of five shots from 200 yards out, followed by five from 300 yards. The bullseye at 200 and 300 yards was a ten inch circular spot, surrounded by two increasingly larger rings, all finally outlined in a six foot square wooden frame. Points allotted were: five for hitting the eye, four for the inner ring, three for the outer ring, and finally two if you hit anywhere inside the six foot wooden frame.

I must say that I found much exhilaration from this new experience. My first shots turned out to be quite commendable: the first one in the #3 ring, followed by the next four finding the bullseye or the #4 ring. I continued to do well, especially from the offhand firing position at the 200 yard range. This was by far the most difficult of all positions, since you assumed an erect standing position while firing, and had no solid support for the rifle barrel. Even the instructors did rather poorly from this firing position. Shots were also fired from kneeling and sitting positions. Much more difficult was the rapid fire segment for both 200 and 300 yard ranges. It went like this: starting from a standing position, the recruit had 60 seconds to hit the deck, get into a prone position, squeeze off five rounds, loading each one manually using the bolt action, then reload by reaching back to his ammo belt, grab another clip of five rounds, slam it into the chamber access, and finally load and squeeze off each of those rounds, always having to use the bolt action to insert each fresh round into the rifle's firing chamber. During all this time of reloading, he was strictly taught to not take his eye off his target number. When there are 38 similar objects lined up far off in the distance, it might take a few long seconds to pick out your number. While shooting and reloading, taking your eye off your target could easily result in picking up the wrong target when ready to fire.

After that, we finally trekked out to the 500 yard range. Boy, did those targets look far away! The bullseye was now a 20 inch black dot. The practice firing sessions lasted for about ten days, finally leading up to the famous "Record Day." This was the day to shine. A perfect score from the assortment of positions and ranges was 250 points, never before achieved in Marine Corps history. But a more remarkable statistic was that, to date there had never been a platoon in which every recruit shot a score of least 195, thus qualifying as a rifle Marksman, the lowest commendable category of riflemanship. Sounds easy, doesn't it? There were also two intermediate prestigious titles more eagerly sought after: Sharpshooter, which required 215 points, and the highest commendable level: Expert, requiring 225 points.

Our Sgt. Harrison spent every day with us on the range and

speculated that his Platoon 148 might possibly have the potential to be the first in Marine Corps history to achieve 100% qualification as Marksmen. He got to "beating the drums" over us, urging us to strive to be better riflemen than we really were. In hopes of sweetening the pot, he went out on a limb and promised that if we were to all qualify, the entire platoon would be exempt from the customary week of KP at the rifle range mess hall, a duty required of all platoons before returning to the main camp. We already revered our Sarge, but now would be even more determined to please him by trying even harder than we already had been doing.

All of us kept a log of our fired shots. I was amazed in finding that I had shot the equivalent of Expert on the first day of firing. That was followed the next day with a meager Marksman score, but then I made Sharpshooter the next three days in a row! As was customary, there was a sort of dress rehearsal to Record Day. It was named Preliminary Day. It was meant to follow the same agenda as that on Record Day. This rehearsal would also help lessen a recruit's typical anxieties of making good on Record Day. I started off great at the difficult offhand position, and continued to shine through the rest of the entire exhibition. My final score on Preliminary Day tallied 216. This meant I had shot at the Sharpshooter level (with one point to spare). Wow! Not an easy goal for this nimrod. My Sarge and the rifle instructor beamed their approval. In hushed tones, I heard talk of my being possibly groomed as a future boot camp rifle instructor here on Parris Island.

Record Day came on November 05. Again, I started out very well at the 200 yard range, and cheerfully moved on to the 300 yard range. The scores were okay for the slow fire, but when it came to the rapid fire segment, something totally unexpected took place as an attendant in the target pits posted the scores of each of my shots. This was with the use of a flag on a long pole, being pumped up and down, and displaying a number denoting the value of that shot. My flags came up reading: four bullseyes, four 4s, one 3, then followed by a red flag, aptly called "Maggie's Drawers." This meant only one thing: a miss, a zero,… a total disgrace! How could I miss the entire target? I was sure I had hit the bullseye. I had been right on target with each shot and didn't buck on any. By two-way phone, my rifle instructor called the pit crew for a recount. These guys could possibly have missed seeing evidence of a small torn hole somewhere on the six foot target frame. After a long half minute, Maggie's drawers woefully greeted us once again. What happened here! The instructor was furious. But I knew I hit the target. Finally, the instructor had the men in the pits check both adjacent targets. Sure enough, one of them counted 11. Plain and simple, I had fired my last round at one of my neighbor's target. Unforgiveable! Obviously I had taken my eye off the targets after I fired the ninth round. At this point, I was called a few choice names by my superiors, accompanied by a volley of threats of never ending KP duty. But, there still remained a very slim chance that I could make sharpshooter if I were to shoot exceptionally well on the last position, single shot, slow fire from a prone position at 500 yards.

Being noticeably rattled by the drastic turn of events, I was now a nervous wreck, but nevertheless had to strive to do better than better. My first shot found the 4 circle, followed by the next one woefully landing in the 3 circle. At this point, it looked like achieving sharpshooter status would only be a dream. Now the threats became intensified, and approached the level of a loss of life and limb and such. It's near the end of the line for me. Nevertheless, forging ahead, the third shot gracefully found the bullseye. So did the fourth, the fifth, the sixth, the seventh, then a 4, then another bullseye, and finally another 4. My total for Record Day added up to 215! In the end, I did manage to achieve Sharpshooter. But I would have shot as a prestigious Expert had I not fired on the neighboring target.

In addition, another drama was being played out, but not on an individual scale. After the score numbers by the total platoon had been anxiously tallied, announcement came through that the entire platoon had qualified as Marksmen. We were ecstatic. We had just made Marine Corps history! Sgt. Harrison was delighted, and we were all very happy to see him so pleased. However, our hard earned award of no KP was not to take place. Much to Sgt. Harrison's chagrin, the upper brass would not sanction Platoon 148 being excused from customary KP duty at the Rifle Range mess hall. The Sarge really felt bad about this and apologized to us. We, in the platoon, just brushed aside our disappointment, and cheerfully performed our duty that week in the mess hall kitchen, knowing that we had just achieved a Marine Corps first.

A week later found our platoon back at the main camp, and also found another feather in our cap awaiting us. Because of our consistent outstanding performances on the drill field, we had been chosen as one of two platoons to participate in the annual November 11 Armistice Day parade in the nearby town of Beaufort. Getting off this isolated island to be among the populace was a real treat for recruits. However, we found ourselves still under quarantine and consequently received specific orders to do our marching with pride, and keep our eyes straight ahead at all times, refraining from scanning the cheering crowds for local southern belles. Nevertheless, the whole affair did turn out to be a totally enjoyable one for our platoon.

We were now getting close to being finished on Parris Island. However, later in the month, Cpl. Huey saved one more brutal act to inflict upon us. We had just enjoyed a full Thanksgiving dinner, and all of us looked forward to having a restful holiday break for the rest of the day. I believe the Cpl. may have been drinking, which in the past had always brought an extra measure of meanness out of him. He called for the customary "Fall Out!" We assumed it would be a lecture, or some similar action conducted in the courtyard. Instead, we were ushered out to the marching field and ordered to run. All of us had eaten heartily and still sported full stomachs. It didn't take long for some to develop stomach cramps, and for others to have the cramps get so severe that it made them double over, some dropping to the ground and unable to get up. The platoon was ordered to keep going. In fact, we were made to double back a few times and ordered to march right over the bodies of our fallen comrades. This episode led everybody in the platoon to intensify their hate for Cpl. Huey.

On November 28, it was time to ship out. Boot camp was now finished for the famous Platoon 148. There was no special celebration ceremony to commemorate graduation. Civilians or guests were not allowed on the base as regulations stated that we would stay under quarantine until we arrived at our newly assigned bases. Earlier, we had all been given an IQ type exam. I scored rather well, and was unofficially told that I would be sent to OCS, Officer Candidate School. I was really flattered upon hearing that news. However, that outcome didn't materialize once the front office disclosed my age. Candidates for OCS had to be at least 18 years old. Fortunately, my good score on the IQ test did put me in with a group of guys headed for Aviation duty at Quantico, VA. Notably, our platoon did execute one last significant deed. As a token for our appreciation for Sgt. Harrison, we pooled our resources from our meager pay and bought him a new wrist watch. Huey, on the other hand, was given no gifts, nor any thanks.

While technically still in boot camp, one last episode occurred on the train headed north to Quantico. While on the train and being escorted in isolation by a seasoned Marine from the Parris Island base, I was approached by a civilian with questions about my tour of duty at Parris Island. After a short while he identified himself as being an FBI agent. The Bureau had received word that our platoon had given our Sargent a gift. This was considered highly unusual. The Bureau wanted to verify that this gift was not coerced. I did my best to convince him that the gift was strictly the platoon's way of showing our deep admiration for the Sargent, and that during training, no events had ever occurred that might have even vaguely suggested any coercion.

When the train stopped in Washington, DC, we were given over to a representative from Quantico. I was now 25 lbs. lighter than when I entered boot camp, and a lot wiser. To fit into this new life might take a bit of work, but this time it will be as a US Marine.

4. QUANTICO - AVIATION ORDNANCE SCHOOL

Quantico was a bustling Marine Corps base, also incorporating a major Marine Corps Air Station (MCAS) for the fledgling Marine Aviation. It held two airfields, Turner Field, where all present air activities took place, and also the non-operating Brown Field which now only housed barracks, warehouses, and the Aviation Ordnance School. The main base also contained the Marine OCS, Officer Candidate School, and was also used as a training ground for the FBI. In addition, a new, elite fighting group was scheduled to soon get started training on these grounds. We met our new leader for the school, MSgt. Henry F. Camper, from Cheverly, MD, a career Marine and true southern gentleman. He had a nice way about him and was very easy to like. The left sleeve of his uniform sported a long row of hashmarks, diagonal stripes for every four years of duty served with the Corps.

Our class consisted of 17 former recruits from different platoons having recently finished at Parris Island. Almost all hailed from the northeast coast states. Those of us from nearby states like DE, NJ, NY and PA could make it home on a 48 hour weekend pass (from Saturday morning, until Monday morning's roll call). Those from New England might have to wait longer and get special passes. We had arrived at Quantico late in the weekend of November 28, too late to get home that weekend. However, an evening's liberty was available almost daily for nearby Washington, DC, a mere 35 miles away. I counted each passing day in pleasant anticipation of the upcoming weekend and that first visit home.

There was a bit of adapting to do in this new life. After having endured the long stress of boot camp, we must all have shown typical signs of intimidation. Just in intermingling, we were prone to instinctively address any other Marine wearing stripes, as "Sir." In the real Marine life, only officers were addressed as "Sir." It was an ingrained habit that took time for us to shed. At first, we allowed ourselves to be pushed around by other seasoned Marines. But, among us former recruits, now all full time students, life couldn't be more beautiful. Contentment reigned supreme over these 17 liberated new Marines.

Saturday, December 06 finally rolled around, and with it my first weekend liberty-pass! The travel plan was to hitch hike the road to my home in PA, and for the return trip to Quantico, take a series of trains. Paid transportation was used only as a last resort, since our base pay had just been raised to only $30 per month. The hitch hiking experience went well. Even though we were not at war, servicemen were still being given special treatment. The first stop was with my folks, now alone since my departure ten weeks ago. Pop gazed proudly on the forest green uniform I sported. Mom had to remark how skinny I had become, and that I should try to eat better. Then it was a quick dash up the street, to where my sweetheart lived. The reunion was a bit awkward, since I hadn't been away very long. As a test of our everlasting love, I had signed up and would be away for four years. Thus far, I had been gone only ten weeks. We were still two kids, barely 17 years old, trying to act like adults. She was still attending high school. The passion was there, but it still existed in the form of puppy love.

The next day was Sunday, December 07, 1941, a day everyone will remember. My sweetheart's folks were very thoughtful of us that day by their spending the afternoon at the local movies, so that we could have their house to ourselves and catch up on everything there was to talk about. I'm afraid I held the floor for most of the afternoon, relating to her all the wild experiences I had in boot camp. The time passed quickly and soon the clock indicated it was time for me to leave and catch my train back to VA. As I was leaving the yard, her parents' car was just pulling into their driveway. Her Dad rolled down his window with rather startling news for me: "Hey Walt, you'd better get back to camp immediately. The Japs just bombed Pearl Harbor and they're calling back all servicemen on leave." Of course, I laughed it off. Some joke! But, when I walked into my parents' home, I found my Mom in tears. The news was true. Her barely 17 year old son was now in the military with a real war to be fought. Thankfully, I did not have to be in a particular rush.

The only commercial transportation that was practical for me to use was the railroad. I had already bought my ticket for the 6:30 train out of Wilkes-Barre which would take me to Reading, PA, where I would change to one bound for Philadelphia. That train would then take me to the Washington, DC station, where sometime between 1:00 and 2:00 AM, I would board the "Reveille Special," a train on the Atlantic Coast Line (ACL) that first stopped at a string of military bases along the Potomac. It then stopped at all big towns along the route to the deep South. It was scheduled to get to Quantico just in time to answer the early morning roll call.

The train trip back brought mixed feelings to my mind. I wasn't even aware where Pearl Harbor was, and its significance in that part of the world. Until now, the general population only worried about the Germans and the grueling conflict in Europe. The train stop was in tiny, downtown Quantico, but my quarters where roll call would be called was on the opposite end of the sprawling air base. To get to Brown Field, where our barracks were, one had first to cut across the big Turner Field. There were no buses running at that hour, which left jogging as the only way to get there.

It was now Monday morning. The whole base was abuzz. Our group from the Aviation Armorer School was promptly shifted over to Turner Field, where all active air squadrons had operated from. There we worked constantly for 72 hours, crating aviation supplies and spare parts for shipment to air bases in California. We ate on the run and took brief timeouts and sit-up siestas until the warehouses were stripped bare. Afterwards, we were all put on the guard duty roster. Every building and warehouse at the vast base had to be guarded 24 hours a day. Tensions ran very high in the DC area, and even though the average serviceman didn't really know what the Japanese military capabilities were in this part of the world, we had to assume their spies were everywhere and capable of committing sabotage anywhere they wished in the USA, and especially at military bases. Normally guard duty would be an easy assignment. You spent four hours patrolling an outlined area, then got eight hours off, followed by another four hours of guarding. You were required to challenge anyone who might wander into your beat and have him identify himself. The exchange was normally cordial, and patience was always extended to the party if he did not readily have identification on his person. However, for the first few weeks after December 07, we guards found ourselves rather trigger happy. If the guard failed to get an immediate reply after barking out his challenge of: "Halt, who goes there?" he was apt to start firing. This happened more than once in our area. However, I remember no incident where it was later proven there was an attempt of sabotage by an invisible enemy. Afterwards, we assumed that these false alarms were probably caused by a passing animal or by a guard's over-stimulated imagination.

The winter month of January turned out to be brutally cold, even for this far south. Staying warm while posted on guard duty posed a serious problem. It seemed no amount of clothing could keep one warm. In desperation, a few guards resorted to entering one of the warehouses they were guarding, just to warm up a bit, only to later be found sound asleep by the changing of the guard. Falling asleep while on guard duty was a serious violation of military code. If caught, one would likely face a court martial. We new Marines were warned to never leave our post, even temporarily, in seeking to warm up. We were told that entering a very warm enclosure after spending a few hours outside in the freezing atmosphere would likely bring on sudden drowsiness. I personally went through this experience. It got so cold one night, that I just had to chance a few minutes for a little warmth. Upon entering the nearby building, I found the warmth actually intoxicating, and suddenly felt myself drifting off. I immediately dashed back outside. The lesson was very convincing and I never gave that move another try.

One day while in our nice warm barracks, we noticed one of our group standing in front of a window and just gazing outside. When approached and asked what he looking at and what was the matter, he gave no response. He only continued staring at something outside. Finally, he snapped out of it and asked "What's that stuff coming down?" It was snowing and what made it so significant was that this young Marine had never seen snow before. He was from Florida and had never before been this far north.

After some time, the new wartime panic did pass and things slowly got back to normal. Tensions relaxed remarkably. It was back to business as usual. Personally, I somehow failed to see how anyone could become so complacent so quickly. Perhaps I really was too young to understand human nature and why you needn't worry about something you couldn't change.

What was significant is that rules for recruits at Parris Island were undergoing major changes. Immediately following December 07, the initial training period was lowered from eight weeks to a mere four weeks. A short time afterwards, the old reliable Springfield 30-06 rifle was slowly replaced by the new M-1 Garand, semi-automatic 30caliber. Later, the training period would be expanded back to seven weeks, and by war's end, recruits would be receiving 16 weeks of training. Also, it was rumored that as many as 1,000 recruits were arriving at boot camp each day. By the end of the war, almost 205,000 recruits passed through the Parris Island Boot Camp.

Soon, it seemed our little group of 17 men in the Ordnance class didn't have a worry in the world. Perhaps we were stationed too far away from the war zone. There were no "Kill all Japs" posters exhibited on our base. We were in school. Frequent evening liberty in DC as well as special weekend passes were rationed, but sufficient to keep us from griping too much. School sessions were always on the pleasant side. Horseplay remained prevalent in the ranks. It was customary for each class to march as a group to school each morning. This was in order to keep a semblance of being in the military, even while performing a non-combat routine like attending school classes. We marched in ragged ranks, usually singing songs that lifted our spirits. We had one New Englander in the ranks named Barnes, who loved to lead all in a chorus of singing: "I am Jesus' little man, yes, by Jesus Christ I am." He was undoubtedly our group's unofficial clown. We were also allowed to smoke while marching to school. One of Barnes' favorite pranks while marching to school was to casually drop a lit cigarette into the rear pocket of the marcher directly in front of him, resulting in the marcher unknowingly leaving behind a smoky trail. There were never any hard feelings generated as a result of this type of horseplay.

Aviation Ordnance School, Quantico, VA, April 1942
Top row: Kelly, #5; Middle row: Barnes, #4, and Brousseau, #6;
Bottom row: Wrinn, #3, and Gagnon, #5

Quantico was a pleasant base, with a good administration, good chow, good buddies and good liberty. It also had a great "slop shute," that is, a convenient beer garden, and a good place for a 17 year old rookie to spend an evening and get a feel for what life in the Marines Corps was really like. In my mind one particular character stood out. He was a rather elderly Sargent, wearing an incredibly long line of hashmarks on his sleeve, ranging up past his elbow. He was a veteran of World War I and had fought in the famous battle of Belleau Woods. His wartime service was so distinguished as to earn him the famous Congressional Medal of Honor. But right now he was a simple, worn out, pot-bellied, beer drinking, old Marine Sargent. The rest of Quantico's residents must have heard his story many times before, but I was all ears when it was offered to me. One day as he walked the streets of Quantico base, a young Lieutenant walked by and the Sarge failed to honor the Lt. with the customary salute. The Lt. stopped, came back and reprimanded the old salt. The Sarge took it quietly, but not without harboring some silent resentment. With that, he returned to the barracks, dug out his Medal of Honor, pinned it on his uniform and promptly returned outside. It wasn't long before their paths crossed once more. This time the Sarge blocked the Lt's path and stood until he elicited a formal salute from the Lt. An old tradition had it that anyone, regardless of what military rank he wore, must be saluted if he was wearing this hallowed medal. Technically, it's the medal that's being saluted, not the wearer. The old Sarge did come out the clear winner in this duel of salutes.

One day I inadvertently created a commotion in our group. I had been sent into DC on a quick errand, and who do you think I ran into at the train station? It was none other than our old nemesis from Parris Island, Cpl. Huey. He had just finished escorting a platoon that had recently finished boot camp. He recognized me and acted very friendly. I also was cordial, since I really harbored no bitterness toward him for how he had treated us. However, when I returned to the barracks and related the news to the gang, there was an immediate uproar: "Let's go get him! We'll beat the living shit out of the bastard!!!" A group of five or six of them raced off for DC, their hearts full of vengeance. When they returned several hours later, they were sad to report that he was nowhere to be found. Again, my young mind prevented me from seeing matters in the same vein as did the older men. I just didn't see the need for vengeance now that boot camp was well in our past.

After a few weeks we finally got to work on aircraft. Unfortunately, on January 31, I came down with a bad case of infected tonsils. The Navy doctor remarked that the tonsils had to come out before I would be allowed any future transfer out of Quantico. Since they were so heavily infected at the time, surgery would have to wait. As a temporary remedy he took a scalpel, and without warning, performed an instant lancing procedure, allowing the diseased tonsils to drain. The sudden act brought on a brief surge of pain, and I reacted by almost jumping out of the chair. Afterwards, I was kept in the dispensary for another six days until the infection had cleared.

Up to just a few years prior, fighter and dive bomber planes were all biplanes, that is, having two wings. Fighters carried fixed machine guns, with the earlier models having them mounted atop the engine cowling directly in front of the pilot, so that the guns actually fired through the arc of the rotating propeller, and on occasion accidently riddling the propeller blades with bullets. To get around this problem, the guns had to be mechanically synchronized to the engine's rotation. Adjusting this mechanism was a delicate operation that we all had to master in Ordnance school. We actually had an obsolete bomber mounted stationary on the ground that still had a functioning engine. With the engine revved up, we students were able to learn the mechanics of how to synchronize the rotating props with the stream of bullets fired from the guns mounted on the engine's cowling. We learned that, on a few previous occasions, a few props had been shot off.

One day during class, we were distracted by a familiar scene of a string of dive bombers practicing their almost vertical dives at a target only a fraction of a mile away. These were Curtis SBC-4 biplanes, too old for combat, but perfect for practicing the art of dive bombing. It was kind of mesmerizing to watch a string of them one by one, fall out of the sky at about an 80 degree angle, sometimes tailing very close behind one another, and then disappear behind the treetops, only to magically reappear some distance away as they pulled up out of their dive. Only on this day, as we viewed the scene, one kept going straight down and for some unknown reason failed to pull out of its dive. There followed a tremendous explosion. The crash left a large crater in then ground as evidence. We were quickly assembled and rushed over to the scene. Only pieces of the plane remained scattered about the crash site. Parts of the pilot's body were found in branches of the trees, indeed a grisly sight.

The dive bombers, since they were usually confined to flying on straight courses during bombing runs, were unable to take evasive action, and therefore relied on the plane's tail gunner equipped with a pair of guns mounted on a moveable turret. Some later models also carried synchronized guns on the engine cowling. These came in handy for strafing targets after the planes bombs had been dropped on the enemy. Then all later models moved these guns to the forward wing edges where all modern planes now carry them. There were very few active planes left at the base after the major move of equipment to the West Coast after December 07. Most new planes coming off the assembly lines at Grumman and Douglas were now single winged ones. The biplanes stayed behind to be used for aerial practice.

In the ensuing months, I managed to make only a few more visits back to home and my sweetheart. Wartime restrictions prevailed as weekend leaves for home and daily passes for liberty in DC continued to be rationed. Wartime guard duty was keeping us occupied. Hitch hiking home on an occasional long weekend would always be a challenge because of the lack of daylight hours.

School sessions, on the other hand, were a delight. I was learning all there was to know about the structure and use of hand guns, as well as aircraft machine guns, bombs, fuses and various ammunitions. I guess there was a lot of student still left in me. Finally, our class was to graduate with each man to receive an assignment to a new air base.

I was pleasantly surprised to be selected, along with three other classmates, to attend Navy Bombsight School in the nearby Naval Proving Grounds at Dahlgren, VA, about 30 miles south of Quantico. However, I recalled that I might have a problem in attempting to leave the base at Quantico. The Navy doctor who earlier tended to my diseased tonsils had told me that I could not leave the base without first having them removed. This was put in my record. There was no time now to get this surgery done. This meant that I would miss out in attending that prestigious school. The situation seemed hopeless. In desperation, I paid a visit to the base hospital and was able to catch the ear of one of the Corpsmen (male Navy medical technicians). I pleaded my case for medical clearance, telling him how important it was for me to attend this school, and that I would faithfully see to it to have the surgery done afterwards. It worked! Maybe he felt sorry for me, thus allowing me to get the opportunity of being stationed at an esteemed Navy base. He probably wished he could have been so lucky.

On April 30, 1942, accompanied by three of my aspiring classmates, we headed south for this mystery school at the very secret Naval Proving Grounds. What would life be like in this new atmosphere? Up to now, it was just one big adventure after another. So far, this very young Marine had everything going his way. I would now be one of four Marines immersed in a sea of sailors. Good or bad??..... Only time would tell.

5. DAHLGREN, VA - NAVY BOMBSIGHT SCHOOL

My Marine classmates were all New Englanders: Wrinn from New Hampshire, John Brousseau from Massachusetts, and Wilfred Gagnon from Maine. Wrinn was a happy-go-lucky chap, seemingly without a care in the world. He did have a first name, although we never used it. He was always known as "Wrinn" to all. John Brousseau, on the other hand, was very young, quiet and serious, almost moody. Consequently he took a lot of ribbing, as we would constantly try to get a rise out of him. He was John, to everyone. On the other hand, Wilfred Gagnon was more mature than the rest of us, and of a different genre, always probing our personalities like he had to find out what we were all made of. He had all the trappings of a psychiatrist. We all called him Willie. In all, we were a well matched group and had lots of fun together. Being the only four Marines in a class with 30 sailors demanded we stick together.

All activities at the Navy base were highly secret. New types of weaponry were constantly being tested here. This also included the boresighting of very large Naval guns about to be used on board battleships and cruisers. The school for studying the famous Norden Bombsight was especially shrouded in secrecy. Once we left the classroom, we were strictly forbidden to talk about anything we had learned in the classroom. Discussions were not tolerated in the barracks or anywhere outside the classroom. This rule was strictly enforced. This was demonstrated one evening when one of the sailors in our class happened to briefly talk about the Bombsight in the barracks. The next day, he simply disappeared. He got shipped out without having a chance to say goodbye to his classmates. The Norden Bombsight itself was very closely guarded and was never left in an empty classroom, or unattended in a test airplane. During any transporting outside a plane, it was always accompanied by an armed guard.

So it goes without saying that all students were always on their best behavior. Living quarters were new and very comfortable. Our chow was incredibly good. The mess hall was situated inside newly constructed barracks, between sections of the dormitories. There was no traditional bugler on the base to sound reveille. There was no early morning roll call, as was mandatory at most other military bases. It was up to the mess cook to wake us up. When he had the breakfast all ready to dish out, he would simply face in either direction and shout: "Breakfast is ready!" The usual response was …silence. Nobody in their bunks stirred. He would then resort to pleading "Aw, come on, fellas, chow's ready!" Still no response. Finally, in desperation, he would resort to his secret weapon….NOISE! He accomplished this by rolling a large metal garbage can lid on its flat side, so that it generated an ear splitting sound as it took a long time to wobble to a stop on the new, smooth concrete floor. Without fail, this always worked. This arrangement of having to coax troops out of their bunks was unheard of anywhere in the services, almost approaching a campus type atmosphere. All meals included several courses, and for enlisted men coming off liberty late in the evening, leftover food could always be found in accessible refrigerators.

There were no big towns anywhere near the base. Fredericksburg was the closest, and it sat 30 miles to the west. No slop shute existed on the base, but there was a handy one located just outside the main gate. So, that's where most of us gathered each evening to have a few beers and shoot the breeze. One could obtain a 48 hour pass for off-base visits with friends or relatives on weekends, but the distance was restricted to a 100 mile radius. My home was in Northeastern Pennsylvania, and beyond the 100 mile radius. I did have a brother, Henry, living in the southern NJ town of Salem, and that location did qualify me for a pass.

And so, one Friday afternoon, armed with my 100 mile pass and eagerly looking forward to spending an overnight with Henry, I happily exited the main gate and hit the road. A main highway bordered the entrance to the military base, but because of the remoteness of the base, no scheduled bus routes went by. So, hitchhiking was the order of the day. The route to South Jersey would take me north along the back roads of Virginia, Maryland and Delaware, to a ferry that made scheduled trips across the Delaware River to Salem, NJ. Traffic on these back highways was indeed sparse, but you would be sure of getting a lift by almost any car driving by. That day I was fortunate to be picked up by an empty bus having just delivered a full complement of passengers from the Baltimore area to one of the fine ocean beaches in coastal southern Virginia. In picking me up he was breaking company rules, and was careful to drop me off as we approached the city limits of Baltimore. I made my way through the city and then was fortunate in getting another a ride that took me all the way to the ferry. Henry was able to pick me up at the ferry landing on the Jersey side. After visiting with Henry and family, I was taken to visit close relatives in Camden. From there, one of the relatives took me across the river to the railroad station in Philadelphia, from which a string of different trains would deliver me all the way back to Fredericksburg.

On a second trip to visit Henry, while still on the highway just outside the Navy base, I was fortunate to latch onto a ride with an Army officer, who was headed all the way for Harrisburg, PA. Even though this was already beyond the 100 mile limit, with still another 40 miles distance between Harrisburg and my home in Ashley, the trip was just too good to pass up. After all, what could possibly go wrong? After the long ride to Harrisburg with this friendly officer, I was fortunate in getting another lift straight into Wilkes-Barre.

This would only be my fourth weekend leave to home; the two other trips being from Quantico. I was still very homesick and each leave was precious to me. I cherished every minute that I could spend with my parents and my sweetheart. This trip would seem like a short one, even though I would have two evenings at home. The planned return trip never relied on hitch hiking, but instead upon public transportation. I would leave the station in Wilkes-Barre in mid-afternoon on Sunday, change trains in Reading, PA, ride to Philadelphia, change trains to Washington, DC, and finally disembark in Fredericksburg, VA. Then there was the final leg from Fredericksburg to the Naval base in Dahlgren, 30 miles to the East. Traffic on that stretch of highway was almost non-existent, since it was traversed only by servicemen and delivery vehicles. One had to either wait for a group and share a ride in a taxi, or hope to catch the milkman making his daily early morning deliveries.

The train pulled out of the Wilkes-Barre station in mid Sunday afternoon during a very heavy, steady downpour. It laboriously made the long uphill grade to the mountain top, then followed a tedious and winding mountain route abreast of the Lehigh River as it wormed its way south toward the next town of Lehighton. The rail tracks closely followed the river, with steep banks bordering on the mountain side, and the swollen, swirling river waters almost reaching the railroad ties on the river side. We learned afterwards that several weeks earlier, this area had experienced very heavy rainfalls causing numerous landslides across the tracks, and some cave-ins inside mountain tunnels. Our engineer approached this sensitive area at full throttle, hoping to clear it before encountering any landslides or possible cave-ins inside a long tunnel that lay just ahead. Without warning, the engineer suddenly applied full braking and we passengers were heaved out of our seats. This discomfort lasted only a few seconds, enough for everyone to get back on their feet. Then there immediately followed a crashing noise, like all hell breaking loose. It was the sound of our train plowing through a large earthen landslide which lay strewn across the tracks.

I was situated in the last car, and as we slowly ground to a halt, we could look out the back of the car, and see that we just barely cleared through the landslide. Shortly after surveying our predicament, we were besieged by another gigantic landslide coming down across the tracks along the same path as the one we had just plowed through. It was so close now, that we could touch the branches of the sliding mountainside. We were held almost breathless for fear that more of the mountain would come down and sweep our train, and us, into the raging river. But, it didn't. When we were pretty confident the landslide was over, we took stock of our dilemma. Then a little hysteria settled in among a few anxious mothers and children. So it fell into the hands of this 17 year old Marine and another young Army soldier, to ease the spreading panic. With an air of invincibility, the two of us proceeded to parade up and down the car, vocally assuring the passengers that we would be alright. After all, "the Marines have just landed, and the situation is well in hand." I do believe that the cockiness and bravado of these two young servicemen did have a calming effect on the nerve wracked passengers.

In a short time, the conductor appeared, and told us the railroad officials were aware of our predicament, and would be taking immediate steps to dig us out. In addition, we were quite relieved to note that the heavy rains had subsided. It was now dark, and we would just have to mark time until a rescue party reached us. The conductor also informed us that the engineer's snap decision to plow through the landslide at high speed rather than try to come to a full stop undoubtedly saved us all from a watery grave in the raging river. If the train failed to stop in time, and we were still moving when we hit the landslide, we would have likely peeled off the tracks and been dumped right into the river. He also told us that the tunnel just ahead was now blocked with cave-ins. We also realized our good fortune in that if the train had stopped just 50 feet sooner, the next, huge landslide would have swept the last car with us in it into the river. The river along side the point at which we were trapped, had now risen to the level of the railroad ties. This indeed was a grim situation. Years later, we learned that this stretch of the Lehigh River is known for its rough waters and is a very popular spot for the sport of white water rafting.

The young soldier and I continued our upbeat banter through the night, and finally at about 3:00 AM, we saw spotlights on the other side of the landslide. In no time, a large track-borne crane appeared and proceeded to remove the debris off the tracks. Then a work crew went forward and decoupled the derailed but still upright front cars and the engine. A fresh locomotive was brought in from the rear, and all the cars still on the tracks were pulled away and slowly brought back to the previous rail station at Mauch Chunk (now renamed Jim Thorpe). On the way, we passed numerous smaller landslides. We sat in the Mauch Chunk railyard for several more hours and into daylight. It was here that the seriousness of my predicament became apparent. I should be back in Dahlgren at this very hour and feared the punitive action that was sure to follow, since I was: 1) AWOL, absent without leave, by going beyond the authorized 100 miles, and 2) AOL, absent over leave, staying beyond the specified 48 hours. I needed to return in as short a time as possible in hopes of keeping my punishment to a minimum. These infractions were probably serious enough to have me kicked out of school and deliver a terrible blow to my cherished career in the Marine Corps.

Since the route we had started to travel was still blocked by additional landslides, we had to use an alternative set of tracks that meandered through swampland, well away from the river. As we were pulling out, we caught sight of our original locomotive which had been brought in from the scene of near disaster. It was parked on a side track, and it was a sight to behold! The entire length of the locomotive, except for a small region at the top front, was covered in mud. It was obvious that this was the engine that had just sliced through the landslide, allowing the rest of the cars to safely pass through. As a further result of the violent collision with the landslide, the cow catcher, a special structure protruding from the front bottom of the engine, had been bent back and up, almost touching the main body of the engine. In the days of old, stray cattle occasionally had collisions with moving locomotive engines, thus earning this structure the title of cow catcher. Its true purpose was to keep the tracks free from all types of debris. This indeed had to be some awesome collision to cause this rigid metal structure to be bent and peeled back. The engine had derailed during the collision, but only after first successfully clearing the tracks for the remainder of the train.

The trip through the temporary by pass was a rocky one. This span of tracks had obviously been out of service for many years. The tracks did not run very straight. Hence, the train went very slow and was constantly being rocked side to side. It took several hours to reach the next big railroad stop at Lehighton. Quickly, our cars were put on the main track, and we finally headed for Reading, PA. Soon after, we were on our way to Philadelphia. My journey then continued to Washington, finally exiting at Fredericksburg. It was now early evening. How would I make the final 30 mile trek east to Dahlgren? The milkman was finished for the day. It took all my resources to dig up cab fare to Dahlgren. I had no choice, since I was now very much into AOL, as well as deep in AWOL territory.

Arriving at my barracks about 8:00 PM on Monday, and incredibly only about 12 hours over leave, I thought, what do I do now? I could easily blend in with that evening's liberty crowd coming in from the slop shute and other activities. Do I do nothing until the first roll call at school the next morning? If I were to be caught, then I would be considered 24 hours over leave, not just 12. I therefore decided to seek out the COQ (Charge of Quarters) and have him sign me in at this particular hour, in hopes of keeping my inevitable punishment from getting any worse. The COQ was puzzled with my request, since at that hour everyone was still free to come and go. He had no idea that I was AOL from the weekend. I insisted without telling him why, and he finally signed me in.

I crashed into the sack without delay. It had been a sleepless and trying 30 hours. The next day as soon as I reported for classes, I expected to be called in to explain why I wasn't present during early morning roll call, and for missing all of Monday's classes. As it turned out, the morning roster wasn't double checked for absentees and the instructor failed to note that I was absent that morning. But I didn't luck out entirely. It seems there had been a special work detail posted for an afternoon work project. The posting was done somewhere outside the classroom building, with a half dozen other students also missing it. This errant group was called up before the "Old Man," the Commanding Officer, and asked to give the reason for their absences. Each man answered that he was unaware of the posting. I wasn't first in line, and when my turn came up, my answer was the same as the others. And so we were all dismissed with a token punishment: that of losing the following weekend's liberty. I couldn't believe this turn of good fortune. I could have been kicked out of school. I truly lucked out this time.

After the excitement from this escapade settled down, I wrote to my sweetheart in Ashley, telling her of the harrowing ordeal on the train, with many passengers (including me) coming close to losing their lives. Her answer really surprised me: this news event never appeared in the local papers. It's hard to believe that the newspapers didn't know about it. I can only assume that being wartime, the authorities felt that this sort of near disaster news could be bad for the public's morale, and was best kept under wraps.

6. THE CLASSROOM

Life in the classrooms proceeded in a much casual manner. There would be no grim intensity associated with the studies. The Norden Bombsight was touted as the U.S.'s most famous and secret war weapon. The program required no elective subjects. All the studies were focused solely on this marvelous, mechanical masterpiece. It was in every sense, the world's first analog computer, albeit a mechanical one. It would be many decades before the advent of computer chips. In its construction, the Bombsight's mechanical tolerances were held to incredibly fine degrees. And cleanliness was paramount. So, in a sense, there really was a strange similarity to today's computer chip development.

The heart of the Bombsight system was a miniature, precision telescope, whose track was driven by gears very much like the ones used in huge astronomical telescopes. A small direct current (DC) electric motor set these gears moving in slow motion. By the constant tuning of a set of double external knobs, the motion of a set of cross hairs located in the eyepiece of the telescope was kept synchronized with the flight path of the plane and the movement of the target. The entire mechanism was held at a perfect attitude relative to the ground by a precision, vertical rotating gyroscope.

With this precision assembly properly adjusted during a bombing run, it was relatively easy to drop a bomb within a 300 foot circle from altitudes of 10,000 feet, or more. The assembly was near perfect in its job of calculating the rate of approach between the plane and target for any given altitude. Errors could enter the picture as one increased the altitude of the flight path since it was possible for the wind to change directions at different altitudes. A second gyroscope, rotating horizontally, established the direction of the flight path, and imparted corrections to the telescope, so that the crosshairs would lock in on the target, even though the plane was either moving across the path of the target, or with the presence of crosswinds.

Classes proceeded at an easy pace. Attending military trade school was nowhere near as complex as college. The subjects were narrow and not too deep. Sure, the bombsight was a very complex device, but the student had simply to focus on learning details and procedures. No complex mathematics or mechanics were required. Except for morning group exercises and the classes, this was really an easy military life. Our instructors were all Navy officers, except for one salty Master Chief Petty Officer.

The student population always seemed content. Each class would go for 55 minutes, followed by a five minute smoking break. Smoking was not allowed inside the classroom, so everyone would be required to spill out into the hallway for this action. This break was generally considered a universal event in the entire military. Almost everyone smoked. However, during one afternoon class, I stayed behind at my desk, while the rest of the class filed out. I had had a very bad case of leg cramps the night before, and was left with very little sleep. I had not as yet taken up the smoking habit, so I just buried my face in my arms, and fell sound asleep at my desk. When the class filed back in after having their smoke, they found me still out. Our Navy instructor that day, Lt. Salsone, had not as yet returned.

Well, my fellow students had a ball, entertaining themselves by giving me a series of "hotfoots." Even these pranks didn't wake me up. After about ten minutes of this horseplay, the Lt. showed up. The nearby students immediately moved to shake me awake. At this, they were stopped by the Lt. and were told to let me sleep. I continued to sleep soundly through the rest of the class session. The next day I was to learn that Lt. Salsone had turned me in to headquarters for the serious offense of falling asleep during class.

His motive was difficult for me to comprehend. The only answer I could speculate was that somewhere in the past, he had a bad encounter with a U.S. Marine, and would now relish in seeking personal revenge. When word got out of my predicament, the student population became rather upset. They were all willing to testify that I fell asleep between classes, and not during class. They all felt somewhat guilty in that this would not have happened had they simply woke me up instead of having their fun giving me hotfoots. Nevertheless, I had to appear at a "Captain's Mast," or "Deck Court Martial." This is a simple form of court martial, where the accused stands before the Commanding Officer while the charges against him are read. At no time is the accused allowed to defend himself with even the simplest of explanations. He just listens to the charges, which are followed by a lecture, then is read his inevitable punishment. Word spread throughout the barracks that I was about to be kicked out of school. This news devastated me, but there seemed nothing I could do about it. As judgment day finally arrived, I stood at attention in front of the CO, ready to listen to the charges and take my medicine. There first came a brief but stern lecture, as if a terrible crime had been committed. But when it came to the punishment, I was astounded to hear that I was simply to be restricted to the base for a whole week, and had to participate with other detainees in digging a Victory Garden, meant to produce home-grown vegetables. What a load off my shoulders!!

After dismissal, my student pals were all happy for me. It wasn't until the next day that scuttlebutt finally revealed what really took place behind the scenes. We understood that Lt. Salsone had strongly insisted on my expulsion from school, and it almost happened, since an officer's word is seldom questioned. However, someone else did come to my rescue, and that person was another instructor, the Chief Petty Officer and long-time veteran, whose word was highly regarded, even over that of a young commissioned Naval officer. My transgression never did appear on my record. Again, this young Marine came through another adversity with very little harm having been done to his cherished career.

FAST FORWARD TO 1951. I have now been in civilian life for six years, having married my childhood sweetheart, and now living on Long Island, NY. I am employed at Brookhaven National Laboratory in Upton, Long Island, about 90 miles east of New York City. My work is in the Physics department, at the research nuclear reactor, one of the first in the U.S. My immediate superior is a bright young Physicist, Dr. Andrew McReynolds. I am fascinated with this science, and spend many hours being tutored by Dr. McReynolds. One day in the course of general personal conversation, I made reference to having been stationed at the Naval Proving Grounds, in Dahlgren, VA. This caught his attention, and resulted in his casually informing me that at that same time he had worked there as a civilian scientist. In the ensuing conversation, I recalled my sad experience with Navy Lt. Salsone. Then McReynolds promptly informed me that they had been close friends. And then he said; "Did you ever hear what happened to Salsone?" After giving him my negative reply, he put forth this account:

Lt. Salsone was on a routine flight one day as a passenger, to fulfill an obligation of spending four hours per month in flight, in order to qualify for hazardous flight pay, when for no apparent reason he fell out of the open cockpit, and not wearing a parachute, he plunged several thousand feet to his death. The pilot was in the process of performing maneuvers, which was likely the prime reason for the flight. The plane must have gone through a roll, and Salsone was obviously not wearing his seat belt (or it was faulty). The incident was listed as a mystery, and there were no indictments for negligence on the part of pilot or others,... a bizarre ending to the previous miscarriage of justice.

After completion of classroom courses, we moved into a hangar and learned to use slow earth-bound Link trainers. These machines looked somewhat like today's forklifts. A driver sat in the rear, manning a large steering wheel in front of him. The student and his instructor would sit on its upper deck about six feet over the machine's front end. Their attention would be focused on the bombsight mounted at their feet. The target was a compact, small, motor-driven bug, about the size and shape of a shoe box. Instead of using the second gyroscope to control the path of the Link trainer in trying to intercept the moving target, the bombsight sent signals to a dial being held under scrutiny by the driver. This dial was the famous PDI, the Pilot's Directional Indicator. The driver's task was simply to keep the arrow centered on that dial, by simply changing the course of the slow moving Link trainer.

In flight, the plane would be under control of the bombsight, which fed signals to a sophisticated electronic system, which in turn operated hydraulic cylinders tied in with cables that moved the rudder control surfaces on the plane's tail. Under automatic flight, the only function required of the pilot was to keep the plane's airspeed and altitude constant. In the real world, if the autopilot were to be knocked out (not uncommon), the pilot would then additionally be required to fly the plane manually, holding the PDI centered, and thereby keeping the plane on course.

After several weeks of this slow motion training on the ground (the bug on the ground moved at a speed of about one mph), we were taken to the airfield runway for the real thing. Talk about tension and excitement! Very few of us had ever been in a plane, so no one volunteered to be the first one used in this airborne segment of training. The Navy then tried being kind to us amateurs. The workhorse airplane for the first part of aerial bombardiering was truly a relic. Its vintage was 1930. Its designation was a TG-1, (Trainer, by Great Lakes Corp). It was a two seater bi-wing plane, entirely fabric covered. The only metal on its surfaces were strips of aluminum along walkways to the cockpit. The radial engine had no cowling, leaving its cylinders exposed. The rated horsepower was 525 HP. Overall, it was so light that two men planted at wingtips could manage to lift the plane a short height off the ground. It needed only about 50 knots airspeed to become airborne. At times when we landed in the face of a stiff wind, the plane hardly moved forward as it touched ground.

Great Lakes TG-1 Bombardier Trainer

And so, we took to the air one by one, to fly around over the Potomac River where our designated stationary target lay. Immediately adjacent to our target range was the Army Aberdeen Proving Ground. We always had to keep a safe distance from there. From his cockpit, the bombardier student would lower himself deep into the fuselage to find the bombsight mounted directly below the pilot's straddled feet, which were firmly planted on the plane's rudder control pedals. Coordination between pilot and student was done mostly by shouting and gestures. After many practice runs, the student got the feel of synchronizing the flight path of the plane. The pilot directed the flight path by following the PDI until such time as the student was ready to take over automated flight. During a student's early practice bombing runs, no bombs were actually dropped, since there existed the possibility of one straying over the neighboring Army test grounds.

One could tell if the released bomb, real or imaginary, was going to hit the target by simply watching the motion of the crosshairs in the telescope after the bombsight signaled that it had released the bomb. As the plane proceeded over the target, movement of the crosshairs became more and more amplified. Any error in the student's synchronization resulted in the crosshairs moving very rapidly off the target. With adjustments and corrections made with the Bombsight, the plane responded by slowly changing course. The plane's reactions to the correction signals from the bombsight were so slow by this old plane that you literally had to wait a second or so for the plane to alter its flight path. After a while, students considered this exercise a piece of cake.

Finally, we were ready to graduate up to a real warplane, instead of a designated training plane. It would one of the Navy's current torpedo bombers, the single wing Douglas TBD Devastator. It had been used extensively in early battles over the Pacific. The famous Navy Torpedo 8 squadron that was obliterated in the Midway sea battle was comprised entirely of TBDs. This plane was mostly metal shrouded, with a cowl-covered engine, and looked very much like a real warplane. At this time, we students were feeling like old salts, and anxious for our turn to take over a real warplane. The Navy pilot of this craft was a veteran and well respected by all. We were to hear that he did have one major fault, and that was staying sober. It was said that he was occasionally observed having to be helped into the cockpit. In spite of this, everyone on the base looked up to him as an expert aviator, and willing to fly with him at any time.

Douglas TBD Devastator, Torpedo Bomber

My maiden voyage bombing run in the TBD started as normal with the pilot at the controls, following the PDI. After a few runs, he signaled that I was to take over the next run with the use of the bombsight-autopilot combo. Setting up the autopilot was a touchy operation. With the controls situated in the pilot's compartment, he then activated the autopilot. Now the big bird was mine. The control knobs, mounted on the Bombsight, were two separate pairs, one for rate of approach, which governed when the bomb was to be dropped. The other set was for achieving the correct course to intercept the path of the target. If the horizontal crosshair drifted off, it meant the telescope was moving too fast or too slow for you to hit the target. If the vertical crosshair drifted off target, it generally meant that wind had drifted the plane off course. In the set of control knobs, one was for a direct offset, a one-time correction, whereas its sister knob changed the rate of movement of the telescope.

Here I was, a little tense, hoping for a good and favorable impression. I approached the target, zeroing right in on it and then was shocked to watch the vertical crosshair beginning to drift off. I had made the last correction in the WRONG direction, and now found the crosshairs rapidly moving off. Yeow! This won't do! Without a second thought, I gripped the pair of knobs and made a quick and large course correction. If I had done that on the old TG plane, I could have whistled Dixie while waiting for the plane to respond. With the TBD, however, I didn't have to wait very long. In less than a second, the plane started to snap-roll over on its side, and for that brief moment, my whole world teetered on edge. A sequence of events flashed by, too rapid to note by this horrified student. I remember the right foot of the pilot (which normally set inches from my right ear), came crashing down on the body of the Bombsight. The intent here was to stomp on a projecting knob that would lock the vertical gyro. Otherwise, the gyro would have gone into uncontrollable precession, spinning around, and with this, sending erratic signals for changes to the plane's course. The signals from this run-away gyro would throw the plane into a spin, or slow roll. However, the pilot's reflex reaction of instantly locking the gyro with his foot while simultaneously switching off the autopilot, prevented the plane from going into a slow roll. Supposedly, there was no known way that a TBD could be brought out of this type of dilemma.

I was devastated. I had been a dedicated student. How could I make such a stupid mistake? The different response time for flight course corrections between a TG and a TBD in automatic flight was rather profound. I later felt that the pilot was well aware of this, always on guard and ready to promptly respond. My heart was in my throat during the entire return trip to the airbase. As soon as we dismounted from the plane, the pilot calmly proceeded to give a stern lecture of what might have been, but at no time, was I belittled or made to feel stupid. In fact, I'm certain that this Navy officer never inserted this episode into my file. He knew that I was a good student and responded positively to all assignments. I had made one bad judgment, but was not judged by this one incident. I will never forget this pilot for his thoughtfulness.

As the school sessions ended, the students were asked to choose the general area of their next airbase assignment: the East Coast, or the West Coast. I opted for staying on the East Coast, whereas my three adventuresome Marine pals put in for the West Coast. Your guess? I was sent West and all three of the others stayed East..... Go figure!

The date is August 4, 1942.

CALIFORNIA, HERE I COME!

PART 2 - HEADING WEST, AND TO THE PACIFIC

7. WITH NEW RECRUITS ON A CROSS COUNTRY TRAIN

On Aug. 4th, 1942, I found myself being driven by Naval ground transportation from the U.S. Naval Proving Grounds at Dahlgren, VA, to the busy railroad station in Washington, DC. This 17 year old Marine was about to embark on his first long journey, completely on his own. Up to this time, my entire 11 months in the service was as a recruit, or as a student. As a recruit, I was under quarantine the entire period, even during reassignment between bases. As a student, well, there too, I was not really able to spread my wings and take advantage of being a full member of the finest military organization in the USA.

For a young serviceman, who had never been on his own, this was a time of experiencing some anxiety. I was handed my written orders to proceed on my own to the large bustling Naval base at San Diego, CA, specifically to the Naval Air Station on North Island. I had in my possession, my train ticket from Washington to Chicago. I was able to relax and enjoy this part of the trip, since I had no other particular responsibilities besides having to take care of myself.

I had the good fortune of having the company of another young Marine, who had boarded the train in Ohio. Carl was good company, and since as we traveled through the night, we found much to talk about. He was part of what the Marines Corps called the line company, and to which the Army generally referred to as infantry. We had the identical training in boot camp at Parris Island, SC, but after that, our scope of training differed vastly. Carl was also headed for San Diego to a large line company base, later to be named Camp Pendleton.

Once we arrived in Chicago, we had to make our way across town to another railroad station that would put us aboard one of the new "super" express trains, heading for the West Coast via a southern route. Having anxiously accomplished this and with several hours to spare before departure time, we wandered around the vicinity and stumbled onto the entrance of a local theater. Not wanting to stray much further from the railroad station, we decided to see the show. It turned out to be one of the old burlesque shows, with a seedy emcee spouting off-color jokes and going through some near-obscene gestures. His performance was followed by a group of rather drab dancers doing their thing. This experience was not very exciting, and we considered it a waste of time. But the time did pass by rapidly, and before we realized it, we were being thankfully ushered aboard the Super Chief, our express train to California. For this long segment of the trip, we had the fortune of assigned Pullman berths for sleeping. We would be spending three nights aboard this fleeting train in its crossing of the vast southwestern lands.

It wasn't long after leaving the Chicago metropolis, that my buddy and I were discovered by a train car full of boisterous Marine recruits headed for their boot camp training at San Diego. Marine Corps boot camp does carry with it a certain mystery, and for these recruits heading into this world of the unknown, their anxiety must have been really cranked up. But here, fate stepped in and provided them with two salty, strapping Private First Class U.S. Marines, in full uniform, who just might be willing to paint them a picture of what kind of life awaited them. Further, they would have us all to themselves for the entire trip. Needless to say, Carl and I ate up this attention. We both stood at 6 foot 2 inches tall and in the peak of condition, since we had just finished boot camp only six months earlier. We carried ourselves almost aristocratically, sort of looking down on this batch of sorry-looking boots (recruits), and maybe lording over them just a bit. I do believe we had fully earned this privilege.

Their probing about what really goes on in boot camp was endless. Their interest was insatiable. They wanted to know more, more, and even more. The questions started early in the morning after breakfast, all through the day, and lasted into the night. Carl and I finally took to embellishing our stories just a bit. Boy, did we get them primed! This crowd of about 50 raw recruits evidently possessed ample spending money, because they constantly plied us with drinks. Carl was a little more mature than I. After all, he was 18 years old, and I just 17. He was able to handle the constant flow of booze with ease. I had almost no experience with liquor, but managed to stretch out my drinks by conveniently dumping them when I felt that I had reached my limit, still being able play the role of a good sport, at least for the beginning of the trip.

And so, with this railroad car full of intensely curious and thirsty recruits, the train was about to pass through the dry state of Kansas. There was no more booze aboard and none to be picked up at any train stop in Kansas. What's more, it was feared that it might be a long time before the train would stop at any big city along the way that did sell liquor. After passing through the remote panhandle section of Oklahoma and into the Texas panhandle, the train came to a surprising stop in the middle of nowhere. The now-sober recruits were very disappointed to learn that the train had stopped only to take on a fresh supply of water at a remote water tower. Periodic water replenishment was essential to keep the steam locomotives going. Our group immediately collared the conductor, and asked when we would be making a stop at a big city. His reply was that it could still be a long way off. So, they put it to him directly: "Where's the nearest place to get our hands on some drinks?"

There was a pause, followed by dead silence. Then he explained that we were sitting right outside the small town of Dalhart, Texas. How far away? "Two miles, maybe, but we'll be spending only about ten minutes here while taking on water." No way to get there and back in time, we were grimly told. A few groans followed, and then more silence. At that, Carl and I caught each other's eye. We both knew what had to be done. This situation demanded some bold action. We hurriedly hustled up a bunch of dollars from the recruits and over the outspoken objections and warning from the conductor that the train would leave without us if we didn't return in time, Carl and I took off like rockets, headed straight for the town's dim lights on the horizon, looking much further away than two miles. It was pitched dark along the roadway. I had second thoughts about this wild venture, as I suspected did Carl. If the train were to leave us behind, we would be AOL (absent over leave), which could put very poor marks on both of our service records. But, these thoughts we entertained only briefly.

In the end, our youthful ideologies drowned out all fears. After all, no task is impossible for a pair of young Marines. Our dash to the town took only minutes. We quickly found the liquor store in the tiny town, scooped up several bottles of booze, and immediately sailed out of the door, heading straight back for the faint outline of the train's lights on the dark horizon. I distinctly remember, as my eyes were fixed on the train's outline, wondering whether we could make it back in time. I don't remember whether I outwardly shared my fears with Carl. That train looked awfully far away. But determination that was learned in boot camp took over, and these two young Marines poured it on. When we finally arrived, the train's conductors were in the process of signaling our departure. The big question was: "Would they have left us out there if we had taken any longer in returning?" Even with the threat of doing this, I firmly believe they would have waited. After all, this was wartime.

FAST FORWARD TO 2002. Many years after the war, and after publishing the story about this escapade, I was pleasantly surprised to hear from a reader who had a similar wartime experience. During a reassignment of military bases, he was aboard a midwestern train, along with a half dozen other Army soldiers, and they had just made a short stopover at a medium sized midwestern town. He and his buddies decided to explore the town during the layover. Upon returning, they were shocked to find the train in the process of pulling out of the station, and were not able to get back aboard. With some apprehension, the group was able to hire a cab and hoped to catch the train before it passed through the next town. He was happy to tell me that they did beat the train and successfully boarded it once again.

Back here on our train ride across the desert, Carl and I were the ones who had saved the day! To our menagerie of recruits, we were great heroes. The booze coffers having been replenished, the young recruits resumed whooping it up as Carl and I frequently exchanged glances with a real special gleam in our eye. In our smug minds we had met a challenge no less than that of swimming the English Channel, or flying solo across the Atlantic. This feeling of accomplishment was like no other that one might experience in his lifetime.

Now, only about half way to our destination of Southern California, the effects of booze constantly being shoved in my face was starting to wear on me. We had two more days and nights of this carrying on to go. Carl was still lavishing in his role, but I was getting rather weary of the constant drinking. So, I started to make myself scarce whenever the opportunity presented itself. Only, it's kind of hard to hide yourself on a train. I would move about into other cars, or stand on the platforms between cars. Sure enough, a scouting party would find me and escort me back to the festivities. I never let on that I couldn't take it anymore. That would be demeaning to the image of a salty U.S Marine. I usually offered the excuse of just needing a little fresh air.

Things came to a head during our last night's ride aboard the train as it coursed across the expanses of Arizona. After realizing I couldn't take it anymore, I decided this was it. No more boozing for this kid. It was getting late in the evening and the gang of recruits were still whooping it up with Carl at their center. I had the porter make down my bed and thankfully crawled in for the rest of the night and the trip. The rest of the Pullman's car occupants were also bedded down. I had just about dozed off, but was startled by mumbling sounds making their way down the aisle. It was a party of the recruits. They were going from Pullman to Pullman, waking each occupant and asking: "Hey, did you see a tall, skinny Marine around here?" I shuddered as they worked their way closer and closer…oh, boy, here we go again, back to boozing. But as they were trying to wake my neighboring occupant, I heard the voice of the conductor chiming in and thoroughly scolding them for their unnecessary intrusion. I was saved! I still feared they would be back later, but I guess they got taken up with their nightly carryings-on, and forgot about the whereabouts of their lost tall, skinny Marine.

And so, I did get a good night's sleep. The next morning a group of concerned recruits found and surrounded me, anxious to hear what happened to me the night before. They were convinced that I had fallen off the train, but were relieved to discover me still alive and not interested as to where I had disappeared. After our arrival in Los Angeles, we were picked up by our military peers, each going his separate way. I was never again to cross paths with my good buddy, Carl. We belonged to two different worlds…..His, the ever tough foot-Marine, where I fit the role of the easy off, fly-boy Marine.

8. SAN DIEGO NAVAL AIR STATION

The Naval Air Station at North Island, in San Diego, CA, provided a pleasant experience for servicemen stationed there. Much like Quantico and Dahlgren, VA, this base was expansive and very attractive. But much more important, it sat conveniently just outside the limits of the big city of San Diego. Living quarters at the base were spacious and comfortable. The Navy chow was excellent. The city of San Diego was indeed a serviceman's town. The local population was rather tolerant of the large contingent of Navy personnel stationed there, and now with the Pacific war gathering momentum, the citizens and the business establishments were treating servicemen with even more courtesy and respect.

Later into the war years, many more military camps sprung up around the city and county. The town became what one might call, saturated with servicemen. But in the fall of 1942, we still had an almost ideal liberty town, that is, where you would want to spend your leisure time off base. We had another bonus, and that was our proximity to town. The air base sat on a large island in San Diego bay. There existed no direct bridge leading into the town, but that inconvenience was overcome with the availability of frequent Navy ferry boats that actually landed and discharged the servicemen at the foot of what was essentially the main street of the city. You just couldn't be any closer. I can still hear the words of the Navy dock dispatcher announcing the departure of each loaded ferry as it was ready to leave the island: "Shove off Coxswain, make Broadway and return." Of course, Broadway was the street at which the ferry landed.

Needless to say, almost everyone went on liberty most every night, except those slated for duty. My liberty buddies were mostly older than I, and as such were more serious drinkers. However, I became a popular companion to have along on liberty since I always managed to return sober. This was primarily because of my youth, since the booze usually made me throw up long before I reached any state of intoxication. So, I typically returned to the base with an inebriated Marine buddy draped over my shoulder. I occasionally was also able to provide a surprise bonus for my pals the next morning by producing a pint of whiskey which I had smuggled inside one of my socks. It was a challenge to pull off this feat. Typically, the guards would turn their focus on only those returning servicemen who were visibly inebriated. My ploy was to make sure I was providing body support for one of my wobbly Marine buddies. The guards would very seldom frisk me. If a bottle was found, the guard would ceremoniously take it behind the guardhouse, and unseen, supposedly toss it into the bay waters. We all suspected the guards were saving the booze for their personal use at a later time. The next morning my smuggled bottle served for providing some relief from any ensuing hangovers. This little scheme did manage to gain me a small measure of popularity among my fellow Marines.

The excitement of hitting all the bars in town every night didn't take long to wear off, which prompted me to find healthier ways of spending my liberties. I decided to team up with a couple of new buddies and try some bowling. I enjoyed the new distraction for a while, but never really got into the sport of it. On weekends, we tried turning to horseback riding. The outskirts of San Diego were rather free from housing or industrial developments and could be considered made for riding. One could simply gallop off in almost any direction from the stables, and experience only rolling hillsides and sparse vegetation. I never did develop the fine art of riding. The horse and I never managed to synchronize the bounce together, and so I wisely selected only the slow and older mounts to ride. It was always a fun group, and we didn't seem to dwell on the seriousness of the war in the Pacific, even though the base was on constant high alert. The airbase, as well as the waters of the surrounding harbor, were kept at a constant high level of activity.

I had two good friends to pal around with at work, and both were clowns: "Vic" Victorino, of Portuguese descent, and Kenny, a real joker from Oklahoma. Both were older than I. At this time in the service, I seemed to have been choosing to hang around with older Marines. This turned out to be a wise move, since the young servicemen usually found it rather easy to get into trouble. Vic was good natured, and took a lot of kidding about his flat nose. Kenny sometimes gave Vic the very uncomplimentary name of "Shovelnose." He seemed to be always cutting it up. On one occasion, while we were all working in the machine shop, Kenny decided to humor us by sticking his chin very close to a grinding wheel in motion while holding a piece of steel hidden in his hand. With his chin in close, he would gently push the steel into the rotating wheel, sending a spray of hot metal sparks out into the surrounding air, and then proudly announce: "Hey, look fellas, I'm shaving." We tended to ignore him at first, but this only encouraged him to get his chin in closer, sending out more steel-generated sparks. Finally, after the third "Hey, look fellas," something unexpected happened. The shop went real quiet. You guessed it! He had come in too close and actually lost a little bit of skin off his chin. We hurriedly hustled him over to Sick Bay and left him there. Later, after getting treated and patched up, he returned to the shop, a much more humble clown. We asked him "What story did you tell them?" In a hushed voice, he answered: "I told them I fell." Well, we all almost fell over with laughter. His humility lasted a week or so, and once his skin looked presentable, Kenny once more resumed being his lovable old self.

I was attached to the A&R division, that is, Assembly and Repair. There were many squadrons of Navy and Marine fighter and bomber groups stationed here. I was considered as being part of base personnel, attached to operation of the airbase, sometimes called the Base Facility. It wasn't as much fun as that of being attached to an active air squadron. Our work was very routine, in that we broke down damaged Marine aircraft to the bone, and rebuilt them. My MOS (Military Occupational Specialty) was that of Aviation Ordnance, denoting that I only had to do with the planes' armaments. There isn't much to the process of rebuilding machine guns, bomb racks, and such. I did however, possess the special qualification of being a bombsight mechanic, but only saw mostly small, single engine combat planes, very few of which carried Norden Bombsights. Those that did have them aboard had to first have them removed from the planes before their arrival at the base.

Almost all our work centered on loads of combat damaged fighter and dive bomber planes that were part of Naval Task Forces involved in the recent great sea battles at the Midway Islands in the North Central Pacific, and in the earlier Coral Sea near the Solomon Islands in the Southwest Pacific. The damaged planes were all single engine, mostly carrier based. We had taken heavy casualties in both these naval encounters, with Midway clearly a victory for us, and the Coral Seas a sort of even trade. A Naval task force is normally equipped with squadrons of fighter planes, dive bombers and torpedo bombers.

In early air encounters with Japanese fighter planes, ours did rather poorly, specifically when pitted against the much feared Mitsubishi "Zero." The bulk of the Navy fighters were Grumman F4F Wildcats. These were rather newly designed planes, meant for use aboard carriers. They were short, stubby, and rather heavy, which resulted in their having relatively poor maneuverability. They all contained armor plate shielding around the pilot and also around the plane's fuel tanks. This added weight only took away a bit more of the plane's maneuverability. The Japanese Zero fighter planes, on the other hand, were light weight since they carried no protective armor plate around the pilot or fuel tanks. They could outspeed and outmaneuver our stumpy F4F Wildcats. In battle however, the Zero was somewhat vulnerable to being shot down when hit by enemy fire. Marine pilots compensated for our Wildcat's deficiencies by avoiding one-on-one dog fights. During a typical air battle, while in search of enemy planes, the F4Fs would spend most of their time cruising at high altitudes while hidden in cloud cover, then swoop down to make a single passing attack at any enemy plane flying below them. After a brief encounter, the F4F quickly withdrew back up into the safety of clouds. The pilots also developed the highly effective strategy by teaming up their fighter planes into close pairs for mutual support.

We also used a truly obsolete fighter plane, the F2A-2 Brewster Buffalo. Although very fast, it too was short and stubby, and lacked maneuverability because of its protective armor plate. Twin machine guns were mounted directly on the fuselage in front of the pilot which required firing right through the rotating propeller. This was the original way it had been done in the early days of air combat. The guns had a built-in mechanical synchronizing mechanism that allowed the guns to fire only at the instant the prop was not in line with the bullet's trajectory. As stated earlier, this style of gunnery was later made obsolete when the guns were moved into the leading edge of each wing, well away from the engine. The Buffalo originally received high marks from the Navy, being their first single wing fighter plane. After the damaged Buffalos were overhauled at San Diego, they were then relegated for use as flight training planes. However, all of the repaired F4Fs were sent back into combat, since we had nothing better at the time. There were new planes on the drawing board at the time, and maybe even some in early production. These would be Grumman's F6F Hellcats, which resembled an outgrowth of the F4F, and also the Vought F4U Corsair, both of which later performed spectacularly throughout the rest of the Pacific war.

Our prevailing torpedo bomber, the Douglas TBD Devastator, performed very poorly at Midway, although earlier it had participated in the sinking of a small enemy carrier in the Coral Sea battle. At Midway, an entire Navy TBD squadron, the Torpedo 8, had been shot down without scoring a single torpedo hit on a Japanese warship. This plane lacked something. At that battle, only one TBD pilot from the entire squadron survived. The TBD was replaced early in the war by the more durable Grumman TBF Avenger, which had earlier participated in the Midway battle, but only as a land based warplane. Both of these planes normally carried Norden Bombsights which were used only when the bombing runs took place from higher altitudes.

On the other hand, the carrier based dive bomber, the Douglas SBD Dauntless, came through with flying colors. This plane had replaced the Vought-Sikorsky all fabric covered SB2U3, which had seen a little action in the Solomons. These ancient dive bombers would further be used only as training planes. Fighter planes had to be fast to compete in dogfights, whereas the dive bomber had to be very rugged. The SBD did its thing by dropping out of high altitudes into a steep, near 80 degree dive, while aiming itself directly at the target. During its dive and pull-away, it was moving so fast that it was literally impossible to shoot down. The pilot was well protected with a sturdy shielding of armor plate. However, in level flights, Japanese fighter pilots found it rather easy to riddle its fuselage mercilessly in hopes of at least knocking the pilot out of action. After repeated failings because of our pilot's protective armor-shielding, the Zero would then go after the rear gunner, who had no shielding. This scenario in the Guadalcanal air battles played out often enough such that the SBDs sometimes ran out of trained rear gunners. The brass then had to resort to recruiting infantry gunners for this special air duty. Eventually, this assignment was looked upon as a potential suicide mission. The SBD also had synchronized twin guns mounted on the engine, giving it some extra firepower, allowing it to often participate in ground strafing of enemy craft on land or sea, and occasionally attacking slower moving Japanese bomber planes.

One Marine SBD, damaged in the Midway battle, revealed about 250 large caliber holes throughout. Yet, this dive bomber managed to successfully return to its base. Investigation of its early history revealed that on Dec. 7th, while parked on Ford Island in Pearl Harbor, this very plane had survived the surprise Japanese air attack. It then saw early air action in the New Guinea area, and finally was assigned to a Marine crew aboard the carrier, USS Lexington, destined for the battle of Midway. At Naval Air Station (NAS) San Diego, after restoring the plane to flying condition, it was decided that it might not be fit to take part in any future air battles. Consequently, it was sent to an Illinois air base to be used in training exercises. Unfortunately, the plane was lost in June of 1943, when it was forced to ditch into the deep waters of Lake Michigan. In the 1990s, it was decided that this plane should be immortalized. A powerful shipborne crane was sent to the crash site and gently retrieved the SBD to the surface of the lake. After a careful restoration, it was given the name "Midway Madness" and assigned to the National Naval Air Museum in Pensacola, FL, where it sits today on display, a true national treasure. The SBD bomber continually kept performing very well in the succeeding stages of the Pacific war, until it was eventually replaced by the new and more powerful Curtis SB2C Helldiver.

A few years ago, the The History Channel aired a documentary on the June 1942 Japanese invasion and occupation of the easternmost and rather isolated Aleutian Islands of Attu and Kiska. This invasion was part of a plan by the Japanese to divert any attention that U.S. Naval forces might be planning in bolstering our defense positions at Midway. Point in fact, the Japanese had placed a Midway invasion at the top of their planned list. Their Aleutian Islands invasion had been left unchallenged by U.S. forces. However, our main bases at Dutch Harbor and Kodiak, nearer the Alaskan mainland were never threatened.

When the Japanese were ousted a year later from their bases in Attu and Kiska, they had unknowingly left us a valuable prize. A discovery was made on July 10, 1943, when one of our Consolidated PBY-5A Catalina Patrol Bombers from a major base at nearby Dutch Harbor, AK got lost while on a regional patrol. To help find his way back to base, the pilot chose to take a short cut which would take him cross the small island of Akutan. While over that island, he spotted what looked like a wrecked enemy aircraft. After circling, he took a position marking and then reported the incident immediately upon touching down at Dutch Harbor. With permission, he returned the next day in his PBY, accompanied by a photographer. After landing in the waters adjacent to the island, they proceeded to slog across a field of mud, to arrive at the upended but otherwise completely intact enemy fighter plane, with it dead pilot still strapped in his seat. The plane's belly was riddled with bullet holes undoubtedly from American ground fire. It was identified as the famed and feared Japanese fighter plane, the Mitsubishi Zero! With the wheels down, the pilot evidently had tried to land the wounded plane on this grassy field. Unfortunately for him, the wheels had locked in the soft ground, resulting in snapping off the landing struts and causing the plane to flip over. The pilot had died instantly of a crushed skull.

Five days later, an American crew returned with a barge, hoisted the plane aboard, and brought it back to Dutch Harbor. After hosing off the thick mud, it was determined to have suffered only slight damage, and with some certainty could be returned to flying condition. This indeed would be a bonanza, since previous efforts to restore wrecked Zeros had never been successful. This project would be given a very high priority. The first inspection revealed an important detail; the plane did not have armor protection for the pilot, or for its self-sealing fuel tanks. The plane was then brought to San Diego aboard a specially rigged freighter, since the plane did not possess typical folding wings.

In August of 1942, the plane arrived at NAS San Diego, and was secretly placed in a closely guarded hangar. Close inspection of the slightly damaged plane revealed that, except for a broken fuel line, the plane's engine was found to be in almost perfect condition. The remaining damage was easily repaired and the plane would be ready for a test flight in late September. Just a few days earlier, I had arrived at the Naval Air Station and was assigned repair duty of Marine planes damaged in the battles of Coral Sea and at Midway. However, as with Marines everywhere, in addition to one's main field of work, there was the ever present obligation of being assigned occasional guard duty.

Wrecked Japanese Zero, found on Akutan Island in the Aleutians

The Zero, after restoration, at the San Diego Naval Air Station

And so it happened that I drew the daily duty of closely guarding the boundaries and entrance of a nearby large hangar. Security was unusually tight. No one was allowed near the hangar at night, and traffic in and out of the hangar during the day was bustling. For several weeks, we all speculated, but didn't have a clue as to what lay hidden in the hangar. Finally, on an afternoon that I happened to be on duty, the hangar doors swung open, and there it was... the wrecked Japanese Zero from the Aleutians! Only, it wasn't a wreck anymore. It was completely restored and looked in mint condition. More important, it now sported the famous star-in-a-circle insignia of a U.S. warplane, instead of the infamous Japanese rising sun. This exhibition immediately drew a large crowd of servicemen. No one was allowed near the plane. Being the guard on duty that day, I remember holding back a crowd while inconspicuously allowing myself to touch the tail section of this prize of a plane. I just had to do it.

What ensued in the following weeks was indescribably exciting. The Zero was a handsome aircraft, having tones of what civilian aviation experts might have considered a sleek racing plane. It carried no armor plate for protection of the pilot or its vital parts, but this reduction in weight added extra speed and a faster climb rate, plus a higher degree of maneuverability. Incredibly, this high degree of maneuverability, when first studied by Naval air experts, was termed as aerodynamically impossible. In combat, the Zero was much respected and feared by our pilots. However, when hit by enemy fire there was a good chance of the plane going down. Our fighter planes were not as maneuverable, but were much more durable. In the final analysis of aerial dogfights, the Zero had the distinct advantage. It was now time to do some serious testing and see if we could uncover any additional deficiencies it might have.

What followed turned out to be a great show. The first day out of the hangar was simply for a brief exhibition to base personnel. Then each day following, the plane was revved up, and gingerly taxied around on the hangar apron area. It then progressed to taxiing along a longer route around the Navy airbase. On about Sept 20, the test pilot, Lt. Commander Eddie Sanders got the feel of the plane, and very delicately took off, circled the field once, and brought it right back down. Each day, he would take off, venture to a little higher altitude and safely perform a few basic flight maneuvers. There was a full audience of spellbound servicemen on hand for each of these daily shows. My guard duty assignment continued for a few more days.

After weeks of testing and putting the restored plane through the mill, the main attraction finally took place: a simultaneous take off alongside one of our Navy fighter planes to see which one would be airborne first. Against the Zero, the Navy pitted their current workhorse fighter plane, the F4F and the brand new and powerful Vought F4U Corsair (still undergoing final structural modifications and not yet fully operational). Neither came close to getting off the ground before the Zero. The Navy then brought the US Air Corps hot, twin-engine fighter plane, the Lockheed P-38 Lightning, into the contest. To the tumultuous cheers of the spectators, the P-38 lifted off the runway well before the Zero, but then sadly failed to keep up with the Zero's superior rate of climb.

Then real flight testing took place in the form of aerial dogfights at higher altitudes. To accomplish this, on October 1, 1942, the Navy's top test pilot, Fred Trapnell, was then brought into these events. For a week or so, Sanders and Trapnell worked together testing the Zero against the F4F Wildcat and the F4U Corsair.

The Grumman F4F Wildcat

The Vought F4U Corsair

These dogfights revealed the Zero to have a marked fallibility at high speed, at which time it actually lost the advantage of maneuverability as it found difficulty in trying to pull out of a dive or in rolling over to the right. Also, the Zero would find its engine actually cutting out as it underwent negative Gs, experienced during specific aerial maneuvers. The lowly F4F could actually regain superior maneuverability over the Zero by twisting and rolling at high speeds. In later studies of aerial events recorded in the Guadalcanal area, the F4F was said to achieve a six to one kill ratio over the Japanese Zero. These test findings were immediately incorporated into the new breed of Navy fighter plane, the F6F Hellcat, just then starting to come off the production line.

The Grumman F6F Hellcat

Although the Hellcat strongly resembled the Wildcat, and was often referred to as its big brother, it was actually an entirely new design. It was bigger, more powerful, and designed to take damage and get the pilot safely back to base especially when operating off carriers. The cockpit and forward fuselage were reset to give the pilot better visibility. Its landing gear retracted the broad, set apart wheels hydraulically into the wing,... whereas the Wildcat relied on the use of a hand cranked mechanism to retract its narrow spaced wheels into the side of the fuselage. The Hellcat first saw action from carriers in September of 1943, and later in November in the battle for Tarawa, Hellcats there claimed downing 30 Japanese Zeros to the loss of only one F6F. The F4U Corsair came on the market about the same time as the Hellcat, but its deep setback cockpit affected the pilots' visibility and prohibited its use from carriers. It also had dangerous stall behavior, and bounced hard when it hit the deck on landing. Hence, the Hellcat was preferentially pushed ahead on the production lines.

Eventually, the Zero would be reduced to being just a run-of-the-mill enemy fighter plane, and it didn't take long for the skies over the Pacific to once more belong to the Navy, Marine and Air Corps fighter pilots, thanks in part to the overlooked Japanese gift to us in the Aleutians.

9. LONG JOURNEY ACROSS THE PACIFIC

A few uneventful months passed with my duties now returning to the routine restoration of combat damaged planes. It was an easy life, with lots of good liberty in San Diego and an occasional even better liberty on weekends in nearby Los Angeles. With good chow and good buddies, I certainly wouldn't have minded pulling a long tour of duty in this region. However, this was to change one day as I heard an unfamiliar voice loudly calling out "Kelly!" It turned out to be a salty looking Marine officer, whom at first I did not recognize, only to realize later that it was Henry Camper, my former affable NCO in charge of the Aviation Ordnance School in Quantico. He now sported the prestigious rank of Warrant Officer, First Class. It was he, who undoubtedly had recommended me for Naval Bombsight School after graduating from Ordnance School.

After a short but friendly chat, he went into detail on the reason for his presence here at this bustling San Diego Naval Air Station. He was part of a special detail of senior aircraft mechanics with plans of setting up an Assembly and Repair base, similar to this one at San Diego, but establishing it as close as possible to the Pacific combat area. This move would free our aircraft carriers that had been relegated to the time consuming task of transporting damaged planes to and from the combat area and mainland USA, and ultimately freeing them for ready use in any pending naval sea battles. Furthermore, in mid-1942, our Country was still reeling from the continuing and overwhelming attacks by the Japanese military. We were desperately looking for some solid ground on which to stand up and start fighting back. A somewhat positive position had been recently gained as a result of the recent Naval victory at Midway in June of 1942, and more recently in September, with our brazen landing of Marines on Guadalcanal Island in the Solomons. Due to our lack of naval power, that operation see-sawed, and for a while was feared unsustainable with the possibility of having to be abandoned. The US Navy was spread too thin across the broad Pacific. Keeping these transport carriers active in combat would certainly add a positive effect to future military operations. Also, having the ability to repair damaged planes so close to combat areas would facilitate their more rapid return to current combat operations.

To set up such an operation, this special detail would require lots of solid expertise. Lt. Camper was part of a group of very senior Marines, all experienced in aircraft maintenance. Their average age had to be above 50, with time in service of 25 years or more. The youngest Marine in the group was Sgt. Jack McMaster, 35 years old with 15 years of service. These experts totaled a mere 40 men, mostly senior non-commissioned officers and a few commissioned officers. With a bit of a glimmer in his eye, the Lt. turned to me with the following offering: "Kelly, how'd you like to come along with us?" Wow! I never saw this coming, but my immediate answer was: "You bet!" It never occurred to me that I would be one solitary kid, just 18 years old, buried amongst this group of old salts. Oh boy, here we go. No more boring life. I'll be now headed for some real action.

I pondered over the fact that I was certainly no aviation ordnance expert. Why would this special detail be asking me to come along? Then it occurred to me that having attended Bombsight School, I could be a valuable asset in the field in providing on-the-spot repairs to the Norden Bombsight and its adjoining automatic pilot. Then it hit me... I might have a real problem, a medical one. I may not be allowed to go on this overseas detail since I still carried that set of rotten tonsils, and had been told six months earlier by the attending Navy doctor in Quantico that I would not be allowed to leave that base without first having them removed. If I had had the operation done at that time, I would have missed the opportunity of attending the prestigious Bombsight School. Remember, while still in Quantico, I had been able to sweet talk the Navy Corpsman into correcting my medical files to state that there was no necessity to have my tonsils removed before being transferred out of Quantico. I got away with it that time, but this indiscretion might have now caught up with me.

It obviously was time to come clean. I marched myself right over to the area sick bay, and informed the attending medical officer that I had left Quantico without first having this necessary surgery done, and that I felt it was essential to have this procedure done right now, before being shipped out overseas. The attending doctor's quick assessment of my throat's condition resulted in the following startling announcement: "I see nothing wrong with your tonsils." Well, I was floored! After being told I must have this problem taken care of before leaving Quantico, this guy tells me there's nothing wrong and I'm OK to go overseas just as I am. Since I was a volunteer, I could easily back out of this assignment, but I chose to accept . It was just too good to pass up. There may never be another chance like this for me.

I now became a member of this select group. We found ourselves with a few weeks left before departure, thus giving the group the opportunity to pitch a liberty together in San Diego. I now had a new group to pal around with. However, my tender age was about to create its first problem. You had to be 21 years old to be allowed entrance into any bar in town. I was only 18 at that point. When I had previously done liberty with my former pals, many of which were also underage, we were usually able to track down some second rate bars away from the center of town that did not do a close check on a serviceman's ID. Hopefully, this would not be a problem since on that day I was part of a group of middle-aged Marines. So, as we filed into an upscale bar in the center of town, the ID checker, noticing all grey-haired men wearing an arm full of stripes and service bars, politely waived them all through. Buried in their midst, I tagged along very closely and found myself being waved through. To our surprise, as 35 year old Sgt. Masterson followed a few seconds after, he was halted and made to produce his ID. He did so meekly, and after finally joining us at our table, he took a solid ribbing from the rest of the old salts. How come this kid Kelly, got away with no scanning, but Jack had to show ID? Jack held this insignificant embarrassment against me for some time afterwards.

On November 26, 1942, our group of 41 men traveled by train to the Treasure Island Naval base in San Francisco to board a newly constructed cargo ship, poised to leave on a voyage to the South Pacific. We were told that this ship had not as yet had the opportunity of sailing out into the open ocean. This would be its maiden voyage! At this time, ocean shipping was in dire need. This was made evident when we found two of the ship's construction crew still working on the ship's rigging, requiring them to stay aboard until their work was finished. After one night's liberty in town, we were kept aboard ship in anticipation of setting sail the next day. All were eagerly looking forward to the exciting experience of sailing under the very famous Golden Gate Bridge in the San Francisco-Oakland harbor. However, most of us had unintentionally slept the whole night through and were very disappointed the next morning to find the ship had set sail during the night and was now far out at sea. We had all missed this once in a lifetime experience.

Our cargo ship was one of the notorious World War II Liberty cargo ships, built by Henry Kaiser. Its name was the SS Elihu Thompson. It was not intended to carry passengers, and was manned by a civilian crew, but had a contingent of 20 Navy seamen aboard to man the six anti-aircraft guns placed along the length of the ship, a 40 mm (1.6 inch) semiautomatic cannon in the bow, and a more imposing five inch cannon on the fantail of the ship. All guns were encompassed by a waist high, heavy metal protective wall. Manning these guns was the single task of the Navy crew.

We 41 Marines were its only passengers. The enlisted men were put in quarters deep inside the hold, whereas the officers were assigned special quarters. This cargo ship was loaded to capacity with ammunition and supplies headed for the battlegrounds somewhere in the vast South Pacific. Topside, almost the entire deck was covered with construction lumber, neatly stacked to the height of the ship's railing. On top of the stacks of lumber were strapped-down five SBD Navy dive bombers. There appeared to be no open areas left on the entire deck of the ship except for narrows aisles for getting around portions of the deck. We were told that the hold also contained several combat tanks and a countless supply of bombs and ammunition. I imagine all westward bound cargo ships were as overloaded as was ours.

My assignment was with the forward 40 mm gun. Two Navy men were permanent gunners at this station. After brief involvements, it was obvious that they were of entirely different personalities. One was a strapping, handsome big guy, bearing some resemblance to the famous movie cowboy, Randolph Scott. The other sailor was a short and older pot-bellied farmer from Iowa. What he was doing in the Navy was anybody's guess. When fired, the 40 mm gun's enclosure in the steel plate structure strongly amplified the sound to an almost ear-splitting level. The pot-bellied sailor found the noise level completely intolerable, and in a panic, hurriedly abandoned his post in search of refuge somewhere below decks. It took some coaxing to get him back to his duty station. In practice firing, I took advantage of the situation by closely working with Randy, taking turns firing this crude weapon. We would aim at the crest of a tall breaking wave, so as to have our gun's tracer bullets ricochet off the wave and streak upwards off the water at an angle, then follow by shooting at the tracers bullets. Randy and I thoroughly enjoyed each other's company during this time. We really didn't miss having our sensitive, elderly farmer around during these practice sessions.

Our ship sailed due south along the coast with plans laid out to rendezvous with a large escorted convoy out of San Diego, also heading for the combat area of the South Pacific. As we neared the San Diego waters, we passengers anxiously tried to catch sight of our appointed convoy. After some time, and the convoy not being sighted, a bit of consternation set in among us passengers. It looked like we didn't get there on time. They had left without us! This was indeed very unsettling. Would we turn back and wait for the next convoy? At this stage in the war, convoys did not gather and sail for combat areas very often. The decision whether to wait did not take long. We were told to proceed alone across these few thousand miles of open, hostile waters and with little firepower to defend ourselves from any enemy encounter. Our two construction workers aboard now had no way of returning back to port, and thus had to accompany us throughout the entire voyage.

To compound our troubles, it was soon discovered that some oil had seeped into our drinking water tanks, rendering the water non-potable. Fortunately, each ship carried an emergency salt water distilling apparatus, although of a very small capacity. For the rest of the trip, we passengers were rationed the meager daily amount of one cup of coffee and one glass of water.

We all settled in for the long solitary trip, knowing that we would have to make it on our own. We realized that we could easily become prey on this seemingly peaceful stretch of ocean. Sure enough one day, as we approached the war zone, we were horrified to learn that a submarine was on our tail. It was thought at first that it was one of ours, but after no radio contact was made the first day, it became a reality that we were being targeted by a Japanese submarine. With all the ammo stored deep in our hold, we could indeed be turned into a Roman candle if hit below by a torpedo. Our only choice was to outrun the sub.

To our relief, we discovered that the sub could not overtake us if we maintained a straight line course. The maximum speed of Liberty ships was reported to be 11-11.5 knots, but despite all our cargo, we managed to maintain 12 knots. The sub, it seemed, could not exceed this speed while submerged at night when an attack would be to its advantage. During the day, it could become a target for our five inch cannon. While submerged, it could only lag behind and wait for night when it had a better chance for a torpedo hit.

During war times, all combat, troop or cargo ships were required to assume a tacking, or zig zag course at dawn and at dusk of every day to avoid becoming an easy target for a pursuing sub. At these hours, it would also be hard for us to spot the sub. The sub still had to get in close in order to get a good shot at us. However, a tacking ship loses forward speed and could be overtaken by a prowling sub. Consequently, our Captain ignored the rule book and maintained a straight ahead, full speed course at all hours of twilight and dawn, thus keeping us out of range of the sub's torpedoes.

As we passed the equator, this cat and mouse game continued for several days. We never did catch a visual sight of the sub or its periscope. Much to our relief, it eventually gave up the chase. I believe its Captain had the advantage, but didn't quite know how to use it. We had to be somewhat of a sitting duck. I imagine he could have been hoping for a mistake on our part, but couldn't make up his mind. Also, he may have been called to join in on a bigger strike in the nearby waters. In any event, we were gratefully relieved. After the war, an autobiography by a wartime Japanese U boat commander revealed that their typical U boat commander found much more prestige in the pursuit and sinking of combat vessels, such as carriers, cruisers, and destroyers, rather than the sinking of cargo and troop ships.

It always had been a hard and fast tradition in the Navy that every sailor and Marine be initiated during a first time crossing of the

Equator. These initiation ceremonies were normally anything but pleasant and could be on the punishing side. However, while under tension during the pursuit, the Navy crew failed to note that our ship had already crossed the Equator. So, we were spared this time, but with the promise that on the way back, when we once again had to cross the Equator, they would get us.

After some peaceful and relaxing days with nothing but blue seas to enjoy, Mother Nature showed she had other plans for us when we suddenly and unexpectedly found ourselves sailing directly into the path of a typical Pacific typhoon. Since there were no weather stations along these vast empty stretches of open seas, we had no idea what lay in store for us. Strolling on the deck would not be safe since the material roped and strapped down could be torn loose by rampaging winds. The only safe place to be would be found deep below decks in our cramped quarters. Except for the pitching and rolling of the ship, and unable to hear the sounds of howling winds and crashing seas, we would not be fully aware of how bad things actually were topside.

A few of us did venture topside for a quick peek at the storm's fury. The sound and sight was almost mind-numbing. The seas were awesome, the winds incredible. I was struck with awe as I watched the ship roll and pitch so extensively that it seemed that the top of the ship's masts would make contact with the churning seas. I imagine that all that heavy cargo stored deep in the belly of the ship was giving this beleaguered ship some extra stability. Most storms in this region typically moved along the course we were sailing, and it wasn't over until the storm actually blew past us. Miraculously, all the strapped down material on the deck survived with only some fabric ripped off the control surfaces of the dive bombers.

Afterwards, we 41 Marine passengers were actually able to relax and enjoy the rest of the trip. Sure, some were seasick during the entire trip. We had our own tiny kitchen and our own cook. But the food was awful and we were perpetually thirsty. There was no recreation aboard. We were unable to do usual daily calisthenics because of the confined quarters and also because our elderly NCOs did not look at calisthenics as a desirable pastime. Playing cards was the order of the day. I got a little acquainted with some of the senior NCOs, who surprisingly let me in. One of them was of Italian descent who was often plagued with an extra heavy beard, with sometimes having to shave twice daily. But after some days at sea, he happily discovered he need not shave for two days. Another old timer that caught my attention was Tech Sgt. Jack Argabright. I don't recall where he was from, but during poker games, his strange dialect had him always pronouncing the word "five" as "fie",… as in "fie dollars." I had been a consistent winner at poker, and when we finally wrapped up the games, Jack became rather upset upon realizing that he had lost money to this kid.

I occasionally enjoyed topside fun with Randy, getting in a little target practice with the forward 40 mm gun. After about three weeks at sea, we were finally treated with the pleasant sight of a few sea birds, seemingly escorting us in the general direction of land. Sure enough, later that day, we passed by some rugged rock outcroppings with sparse vegetation. This land turned out to be a tiny, easternmost island in the chain of the five islands of Samoa. Finally, we were told that our destination would be the main island of Tutuila, American Samoa.

The next day, the large outline of this long mountainous island loomed large on the horizon. Soon we sailed into the spacious, deep water, beautiful harbor of Pago Pago. There, we were greeted by a flotilla of outrigger canoes, full of cheerfully waving natives, chanting a familiar greeting: "Hai Kai, Melingi," which we later discovered translated literally into "You eat shit, Marines." We were relieved, odd as it was, to learn that this greeting was cordial, and not meant in any way to be derogatory. Without further ceremony, we disembarked and were hustled aboard trucks and hauled a distance of about ten miles down the coast to our new home at an airfield, but one much unlike the one we had left a few weeks ago in San Diego.

The date is December 15, 1942.

WE MADE IT!

WELCOME TO THE SOUTH PACIFIC.

PART 3 – OVERSEAS: SAMOA, AND ON TO TARAWA

10. SETTLING IN

The Samoa Islands are located about half way along a chain of islands in the South Pacific between Hawaii and the east coast of Australia, and formed the last remaining air–sea war time route between those two areas. This vital chain of seaports and airbases also included the large islands of Fiji and New Caledonia. After a mighty sweep by Japanese forces in conquering Allied bases spread along the Eastern and Central Pacific, much concern existed over the possible loss of any additional territory along this last remaining supply line to Australia.

Previous to the Pearl Harbor attack, reinforcements had been trickling into Tutuila, the main island in the American Samoa group, and the most valuable of the three major Pacific island bases remaining along this sea- air route. A contingent of 443 men of the 7th Marine Defense Battalion had already arrived here in March of 1941. They were the very first Marine troops brought into the Pacific's southern hemisphere. They brought with them eight 155 mm guns, relics of WW I, all virtual museum pieces which had been in use on the grounds of Marine Corps training centers at Parris Island and San Diego. By 1941 standards, these relics might be considered rather unsafe to fire.

The Battalion also implemented and trained a militia of local native men, instructing them in the use of Springfield rifles. We were surprised to later learn that the native men in the militia were much sharper in picking up the art of drilling and marching than were the average US Marine. Building defense positions around the Pago Pago harbor was assigned a high priority. The island's native men were also being trained to operate trucks, bulldozers and other special machinery used around the harbor. In recent defense of the harbor, the US Navy had taken the precaution of mining the harbor and its approaches. On January 11, 1942, a lone Japanese submarine brazenly surfaced outside the Pago Pago harbor of American Samoa, and for ten minutes lobbed shells into the harbor area, inflicting little damage, with only a few minor injuries to the American and native guards.

Even though damage was minimal, this incident created cause for concern.

SAMOA ISLANDS

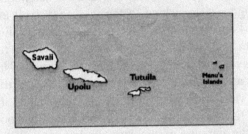

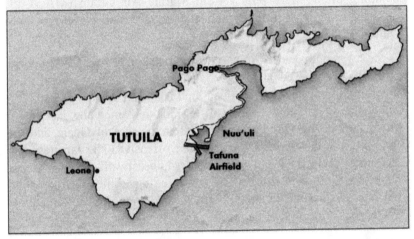

On January 20, 1942, some 5,600 men of the 2nd Marine Brigade arrived on Tutuila. They had been privileged in having an escort fleet of two American aircraft carriers and warships to chaperone them across the open Pacific. This was a tribute to the importance of keeping the Samoan base out of Japanese hands. A new battalion was organized and immediately proceeded to set up anti-aircraft positions in the hills around the harbor. Much effort was initiated to set up defenses along the entire perimeter of the island. This new battalion then replaced the existing 2nd Brigade, which was sent to shore up defenses on the neighboring island of British Samoa, called Upolu.

In late April, 1942 Major General Charles F.B. Price arrived to take over command of the Samoan Defense group. Secret orders had come down a few weeks previous that mandated establishing strong defensive positions on all neighboring islands, including neighboring British governed Upolu, and its neighboring and lesser developed bigger sister island to the west, Savaii. It also included a nearby little known outpost of French-governed Wallis Island, only 300 miles to the west. General Price was later to receive the outstanding award of The Legion of Merit from the Navy's Admiral Nimitz. This award was often given to commanding officers in battle zones, those verified to have exhibited a high degree of leadership. It read, for: "His outstanding work in successfully coordinating and supervising the defense of the Samoan Islands." With the defenses spread so thinly and broadly about the islands, some servicemen, including pilots, were pulled from Marine Air Group (MAG) 13, retrained as defense infantrymen and pressed into service to help guard the islands.

A month earlier it was learned that the Japanese Imperial Army had approved plans for an offensive against these three remaining South Pacific American-held islands; Samoa, Fiji and New Caledonia. In addition to Hawaii, Samoa remained the last major Allied port in the vast Pacific, this after the loss of Guam and the Philippines at the onset of the Japanese offensive. The Japanese had cautiously decided to halt their rapid southeastward advance across the North Central Pacific, when just three days after Pearl Harbor, they occupied islands in the Gilberts, located on the equator and about 1,400 miles northwest of Samoa.

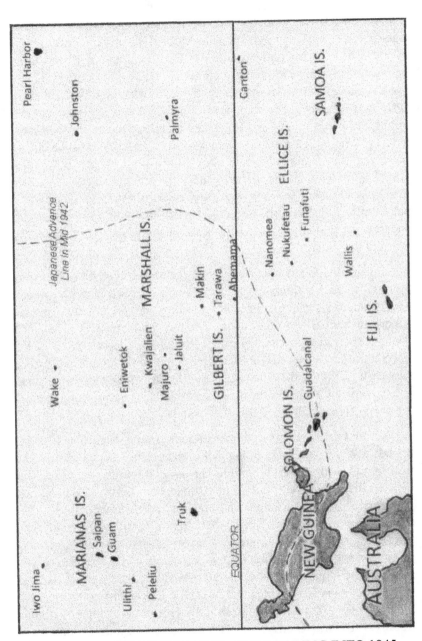

THE PACIFIC WAR THEATER, 1942 LEADING INTO 1945

Soon after, other Marine Corps units started arriving on Tutuila. These were the First Raider Battalion, a Balloon Barrage Battalion, several other Battalions, a Mobile Hospital, as well as half of a Naval Construction Battalion (CB). The number of incoming personnel now totaled almost 8,000 men. One of these Battalions was assigned to a secret mission, that of securing nearby Wallis Island, since it was feared the then governing French Vichy government might be hostile to any and all Allied activities in the Samoan area. On May 27, 1942, assault companies of the 3rd Marine Brigade landed on Uvea, the main island in the Wallis atoll, about 300 miles northwest of Tutuila. Surprisingly, they encountered no resistance, but the units continued occupation of the area, also setting up defenses on neighboring isles as well. In early August, the units were pulled out and sent to join in the heavy fighting on Guadalcanal, some 1,900 miles to the West.

In July, the ever cautious Japanese high command canceled its proposal to start a campaign to take Samoa, Fiji and New Caledonia, and decided instead to concentrate efforts on taking the strategic American held island of Midway, not too far west of the Hawaiian Islands. Later that month, 24 miles east of Tutuila, a converted US troop ship had survived an attack by a Japanese submarine. In late August on Tutuila, the first wounded Marines from the Guadalcanal and Tulagi campaigns in the Solomon Islands arrived for treatment at the newly finished 300 bed mobile hospital.

In late November, 1942, Captain Eddie Rickenbacker, the famed WW I flying ace, along with seven other passengers, while traveling aboard an old B-17 from Hawaii and on the way to the war zone in the Solomons, became lost somewhere between Hawaii and the remote island of Canton, and crashed in unknown waters. After three harrowing weeks aboard small life rafts, all were found and rescued by American float planes. They were first brought to bases in our recently occupied Ellice Islands, where they received emergency medical attention, then subsequently transported by one of our two PBYs from American Samoa and brought back for further treatment at Samoa's new 300 bed hospital. In early December, another battalion from New River, NC arrived on Tutuila, poised for jungle training.

On December 15, 1942, the SS Elihu Thompson with its detail of 41 seasoned Marine Corps aircraft maintenance experts quietly sailed into the famed Pago Pago harbor. It was great to once again experience the feeling of firm ground under one's feet. However, a few Marines were shocked to discover that some of their previous symptoms of seasickness had returned. The sudden change from a constant rocking ship to solid ground is somewhat analogous to the original experience of seasickness soon after boarding a rocking ship. These few men were also ones who had been dreadfully sick for the majority of the cross-ocean voyage. This time, fortunately, their sick feelings did not last as long. Thankfully, I was not among those stricken in either case.

The harbor at Pago Pago was a deep and excellent one, but with limited modern facilities. Surprisingly, it held a branch of the Bank of America. The natives proved to be quite intelligent and quickly learned the complex tasks of truck driving and operation of the harbor cranes. They became useful laborers for our government and delighted in becoming wage earners. At times, it was surprising to observe a line of native workers in front of the bank waiting to deposit their wages. It was almost comical in that few goods were available for purchase in this area. Their lifestyle made them rather independent from the outer world. We were told that they were fascinated with the typical American merchandise catalogs and took much pleasure in ordering gadgets like sewing machines, even though electricity was not available in the outlying villages.

The utter mountainous terrain of this 27 mile long island strongly affected the diet of its inhabitants. There were no farms here, nor any domestic animals. Their protein came from the bountiful supply of fish found in the surrounding coastal waters. The native men were very deft in their approach to catching fish. Natives could often be seen floating face down in the shallow coastal waters, spearing fish as they swam by just below the surface. There were abundant fruit trees with bananas, coconuts, breadfruit and papaya available for harvesting at almost any time of the year. The only finished and maintained road on the island was the one that hugged the coastline between the harbor and the airport at Tafuna. While most of the large villages hugged the coastline, there were many smaller ones scattered throughout the island's interior. The greater population was confined to the immediate Pago Pago harbor area. It was an ideal harbor, with its high, sheltering and encompassing mountains, and its deep waters.

This was to be our new home, 4,800 miles from California, 2,600 miles from our stronghold at Hawaii, and 1,400 miles southeast from our adversary, the Japanese Army, now firmly entrenched on Tarawa, the main island in the Gilbert Islands chain. It felt great to be on firm ground once more and free from all further perils of weather and enemy submarines prowling about the open seas of the Pacific Ocean. We felt very safe here, thanks to the very recent influx of thousands of Marines and the amassing of weapons.

Marine Corps Airfield at Tafuna, Tutuila - 1942

The airport at Tafuna had been under expansion for civilian use when the war broke out, at which time the US government took over and immediately ratcheted up the pace of construction. The first short emergency runway was completed in early April of 1942, and could only be used by our small and nimble fighter planes. Construction of a much longer runway was immediately started. The first light warplanes from Marine Air Group, MAG-13, arrived shortly after. However, overall construction still did not please the military brass. A meeting of high officials took place shortly afterward which resulted in the decision that, since too little progress was being made with the existing construction, emphasis changed from the building of large hangars and utility shops to small, scattered and more easily camouflaged structures. It took until June of 1942 to complete the new, highly desirable mile-long runway. This air strip, made up of dredged and compacted coral would now lie across the full width of the shallow lagoon. It also provided a much safer landing path for incoming planes, since it stretched along a path almost parallel to the adjacent mountain range. Several dozen fighter and dive bomber planes soon followed and a suitable air defense was organized for the surrounding area.

In the villages west of the airport, very few of the native population had ever encountered a white person. Recently, a small airport had been carved out on the side of the mountain about another ten miles further west, in an area called Leone Point. It was built as an emergency landing field for only smaller fighter planes, but had to be abandoned after it was determined impractical and dangerous for any type of plane landings. It was also difficult to reach by road. One day, a visiting Army Air Corps bomber pilot, mistakenly took it for the main airport, and landed his B-26 medium bomber on this short runway. This plane possessed scanty wing lift, and was inherently heavy. It was not able to successfully take off from this short runway, even if stripped of all armament and with almost empty fuel tanks. So it was dismantled into smaller sections and painstakingly brought down to the main airport. There it was re-assembled, never again to see action on the front lines. It was eventually relegated to the mediocre task of occasional cargo runs and to fly aerial tow targets on which our local fighter plane pilots could practice their aerial skills.

The facilities of the air station at Tafuna were very basic. Our outfit was designated as MCAF, "Marine Corps Air Facility in the Field." There were a few small office buildings, all located near the water's edge. Our amenities were almost nil. Our PX was the size of an average living room, dispensing only the bare necessities like soap, toothpaste, and writing materials. There was no slop shute, nor any other place to buy a beer or a soda, or even a hamburger. There was no library. There were occasional movies, all held in a phased out, massive balloon barrage hangar, in which all seats were make-shift, like crates, planks, and even dummy bombs. This hangar also held church services. We were never graced with a visit by any USO troupe, although in July of 1943, we did once catch a glimpse of First Lady Eleanor Roosevelt accompanied by then Secretary of the Navy, Frank Knox, as they whizzed by in a command car while on a brief inspection visit on Tutuila and other island bases in the combat zone.

Prior to arrival of US military forces, the general area of Tafuna was naturally rich with banana and breadfruit trees. A major effort was made during construction, and afterwards, to keep these areas intact for harvesting by the natives. As soon as we arrived, our very first desire was quenching our thirst, since we had been rationed two cups of drinking water aboard ship throughout our entire sea journey of 18 days. The water here in Tafuna was being dispensed out of canvas Lister bags (leather-like pouches), and since it was treated with iodine pills, had a very unpleasant taste. With the arrival of more and more troops a few months later, the military brass saw fit to quickly construct a fresh water dam high up in the adjoining mountain range, which experienced rather high annual rainfall. This fresh water was then piped into selected buildings in the immediate areas of the airbase. The water was also piped into our almost modern latrine structure which was built on stilts and perched over the lagoon water's edge. It also contained sinks with faucets and running water, urinals and even sit-down commodes and above all, real showers. Sewage treatment was not a problem. Nature took care of that. The tidal flushing action in the lagoon waters kept the area pleasantly fresh. These facilities were crude, but very functional. We were also blessed to have electricity in all work buildings and living quarters, just not the latrine.

Our living quarters were all prefabricated eight man wooden huts located just inside the canopy of the jungle so as to be easily camouflaged from the air. However, all the buildings in the main compound were out in the open. Each hut, called a Fale, (pronounced "fallee") had a regular entrance door, but no working windows. The bunk beds were stacked in twos, each in one of the four corners. The upper beds did enjoy lots of fresh air because the periphery of the hut held screening along the entire upper bunk level. This, as compensation for having to climb up and in and out of the sack. To shield from getting drenched by the frequent downpours of rain, a canvas curtain stretched around the fale's outside wall and was easily drawn across the screened section. This setup worked rather well. We were also endowed with mosquito netting for over each of our bunks, which we often chose not to use.

Kelly outside his fale, 1943

Each fale had a generous sized table placed in its center, and was used for tasks such as writing letters and playing cards. Our roofs were made of corrugated steel sheets, which produced a highly undesirable loud and disturbing noise whenever it rained hard, which it did nightly, or, when a coconut unexpectedly dropped from high out of one of the tall trees that overlooked the camp. This effect was always extra disturbing late at night as it produced a really loud bang, followed by a thumpity-thump noise as the coconut then rolled down the corrugated tin roof.

Like any kid in a new playground, our first thoughts turned to exploring our new environment and its abundant native food. Coconuts got first focus of our attention. Most of us had already tasted one at some point in our lives. Here was an opportunity to have a real fresh coconut, right off a tree. The trees all bore abundant fruit, but only at their very tops. Retrieving the fruit looked rather difficult, since the tree had no protruding limbs along its main trunk. However, there were plenty of fallen coconuts spread about on the nearby ground. Some of us, perhaps still feeling the effects of water restrictions imposed on us during our long voyage, wasted no time in crudely trying to hack open the coconuts and gorging on the milk. A few servicemen, already based here for a while, watched in silence as this orgy unfolded. If only they had warned us... That evening, it started: A steady stream of newly-arrived Marines hastily barreling down the path to the latrine. It seems that only a small amount of ripe coconut milk will give you a decent bowel movement. But the quantity we had consumed was enough to give each of us a real bad case of the runs. Fortunately, this affliction lasted for only a day or two. After it was over, we would then enjoy the pleasure of silently standing by as newly arriving troops experienced a similar experience. We soon learned that the right thing to do was to eat the meat of a ripe coconut, but drink the milk of only a green one.

Not long after our recovery, there still stood the challenge of retrieving the safer-to-drink coconut juice from the fruit still high up on the tree. The only way to get that done was to shimmy up one of these skyscrapers (they averaged 30 feet high). The natives did it with much ease. Our approach was not their tried and proven way, which was by hopping up bunny style and digging in using the help of a rope tied across their ankles. No, we tried hugging the tree with our hands and with our legs wrapped around it, and to slowly pull our bodies up, a little bit at a time. Many of the tougher Marines made vain tries to climb high enough to reach the fruit bunched up high in the canopy. They failed one after another, so it was up to this smart-ass young Marine to give it a try. I may have been short on strength, but made up for it with determination. Making my way up, I almost gave up several times, but somehow made it to the top and with one wild swipe of my hand, just barely succeeded in dislodging a few coconuts. Unfortunately, this arm motion caused me to lose my grasp around the tree. It seemed that I had used every bit of my strength to make it to the top, and was left short in what was needed for a slow descent. Down I slid, somewhat out of control and much too fast, all the way to the bottom. My reward for that day's great achievement was the loss a good bit of surface skin from my chest and the inside of my arms and legs. And hero that I was, I found it difficult for a week afterwards to stand up straight. I now knew how it felt to be more a fool than a hero.

Use of the latrine could be a bit of drudgery, since it was situated about 100 yards walking distance from our fales. From the start, we were warned about fungus diseases being prevalent in tropical climates. American Samoa lies on the 15th parallel, similar to Southern Cuba. The area was always very humid and conducive for fostering mold and fungus. Taking daily showers was a must. When hiking down the jungle trail from our huts to the latrine to use the showers, we would typically go bare-chested and bare-bottomed, but with a towel wrapped around our waist. We made sure to protect our feet by wearing a pair of wooden "klaks". Walking bare footed was a certain way of acquiring a good case of foot fungus. Our woolen green uniforms had to be discarded a short time after our arrival. We certainly didn't miss them, since there were no liberty towns within 1,000 miles of us. The ever-present mold problem of stored clothing was very effectively solved with the simple installation of a 60 watt light bulb in each of our metal clothes cabinets. This light was left on 24 hours a day. With that, everything inside our cabinets stayed nice and dry and free of mold.

It was very common during the day, when not at work at the airstrip, to encounter a group of female natives treading their way along the jungle paths, gathering bananas and breadfruit for daily consumption. They were always cheerful amongst themselves, but cautiously friendly when in our company. The Marines were always treated as welcome guests. Male natives never stooped to menial tasks such as fruit gathering. They spent their day spear fishing for food and other more manly pursuits and were seldom seen in the company of female workers. On one particular occasion, one of our more mature Marines, named Copeland, was walking down the trail to the latrine with only a towel wrapped around his waist, when a group of young native girls appeared along the same path, coming from the opposite direction. They were, as usual, a happy bunch, just chattering and laughing and completely ignoring the approaching Copeland, whom they had to pass along this narrow path. As the last native girl passed by him, she deftly reached over, grasped a corner of the towel draped around his bottom, and whipped it off. A group of us had intently been following this scene because at this time, we were not used to having natives among us and didn't know quite what to expect. The native girls now all began to shriek in the sheer pleasure of the moment, by taking advantage of his exposure and gleefully pointing at his genitals. Poor Copeland! He was so embarrassed. He desperately tried to retrieve his towel by approaching the girl who had stolen it. But she in turn, would stand her ground and reach out as if to grab at his genitals. This standoff lasted for a few minutes much to the delight of the native girls and, of course, we spectator Marines. Finally, after considerable pleading, Copeland was rewarded with the return of his towel. Afterwards, he had a hard time living down this episode.

We young Marines had a hard time adjusting to an environment with native girls often parading about during any part of the day. But daring we were…to a point. All natives, both men and women wore lava lavas, which were simple one-piece wrap around garments with likely no under garment. Up until recently, those girls living away from the main town and harbor of Pago Pago, customarily walked around bare breasted. As more American troops moved into any new area, the U.S. Navy always followed with a directive to have them keep their bosoms covered. The Navy would get things started by issuing them regular Navy tee shirts. However, we soon found that they loved having their picture taken and would gladly remove their chest cover to proudly pose for a snap shot. Some of us possessed cameras, but unbeknownst to the natives, the cameras contained no film. For security reasons, taking photos of any kind on the island was strictly forbidden. We young warriors were privy to an occasional fake inspection of a local female's bosom by simply asking if they would like their pictures taken. This practice abruptly ended after the girls finally caught onto our little scheme.

After a short period of time, the younger girls discovered the pleasing Western style of wearing dresses instead of their customary lava-lavas. However, the wearing of underwear did not immediately follow. On one particular occasion, as a young dress-wearing girl was passing by a group of us, we shouted out… "NO PANTS!" We usually got an immediate coarse reply in Samoan, but when the No Pants was repeated, she became rather annoyed. As soon as there was sufficient safe distance between us, she flipped up her skirt in the back, slapped her bare behind, and then laughingly ran off to safety. This game provoked much laughter among the spectators, and it seemed that the victim may also have enjoyed the game a bit.

This little incident sort of laid the ground work of how we were to treat our hosts, and they, us. The method of self-government of the natives was simple but effective. Each village was rigidly ruled by an elder, who made all important decisions, even to the point of who should marry whom. Couples were not necessary monogamous. Children could belong to different parents, and were cared for on almost a community basis. There were no objections by the chiefs or elders, against fraternizations between the native girls and the Marines. Native girls having babies by Marines was not entirely discouraged as long as that girl was not promised to a male native. The sex part of this philosophy seemed not to play an important part. Having sex was just not that big a deal to the native population.

Life inside the eight man fale huts soon became rather routine. These prefabricated wooden buildings were scattered about along the edge of the jungle. Natural vegetation was always required to remain in place so that the small buildings would remain relatively invisible from the air. Fortunately, we experienced no enemy air raids, since we were too far from the front lines. When night time fell, each fale would be occupied by all its inhabitants, since there was no other place to hang out. We had no radios or similar distractions, so the nightly activity usually ended up with us playing card games, such as poker and black jack. Mosquitoes were especially vicious after dark, and we found welcome haven inside our screened-in fales. There was another small nuisance however, and that was what we called coconut bugs, which were small enough to crawl through the screens. They had a very hard body and were hard to squash dead. They didn't bite but were a distinct nuisance because of their vast numbers. They were attracted to the lamp hanging over the blanket covered table. Instead of spraying repellent, we effectively kept them in check by simply keeping everyone present at the table busy smoking cheap, smelly green cigars, non-stop.

Since there was no place to spend our monthly paychecks, we were allowed to draw any amount of pay, or just enough for daily needs. This reflected in our card games. All the games centered about payday poker as well as payday black jack. Stakes were typically low scale, since we played every night. It was primarily meant as a way to pass the time. When payday came around, everybody squared up their existing debts. However, specifically on payday, there was a lot of attention focused on high stakes crap games, usually involving a few thousand dollars.

As a rule, the older Marines faithfully sent their winnings to their wives and families back home, along with the normal monthly pay they didn't use. Yours truly did very well playing poker each night, and would often accrue a nice bundle of cash by the time payday rolled around. Instead of sending these winnings home, I took them into an ensuing hot craps game, in hopes of coming out a big winner. On one occasion, I got on a real hot streak by rolling a series of unbroken "naturals". This means rolling a 7 or 11, an instant winner. I cleaned out just about every one of the other players except for one, a chap named Vito. My winnings at this point were in the vicinity of $2,000, a real tidy sum, considering a Private's base pay at that time was $30 per month.

So, it settled down to a contest between the two of us. Since we were all rather new, we didn't really know each other. But Vito carried the airs of a Mafia character and you knew right from the start, that you didn't treat this guy casually. He knew how to twirl the dice, and seem to come up with only good numbers. And to no one's surprise, it didn't take long for him to systematically relieve me of all my winnings. I was now broke and the game ended on that note. During the contest, I found myself accruing too many dollar bills to hold in my hand, so I had to resort to stuffing them into all my pockets. During a following morning's self-inspection, I was delighted in finding two $20 bills stuffed in my rarely used watch pocket. Considering I had entered this big crap game with only $20, and ended with $40, I really did come out ahead for the night!

I had not challenged Vito on his unorthodox method of rolling the dice, and that turned out to be a good thing. After all, what would an 18 year old know about twirling dice? A few weeks later, an argument took place in our fale as to who was in charge. Technically, it was Sgt. Amos Baccus, a rather refined gentleman who had no penchant for playing cards, but rather preferred to spend the evenings reciting poetry and singing old ballads, such as:

"In days of old, when knights were bold, and Barons held their sway, a warrior bold with spurs of gold sang merrily his way, sang merrily his way.

My love is young and fair, my love hath golden hair, and eyes so blue and heart so true, that none with her compare.

*So what care I though death be nigh, I'll live for love or
die. So what care I though death be nigh, I'll live for love
or die.*

*So, this brave knight in armor bright rode gaily to the
fair. He fought the fight, but 'ere the night, his soul had
passed away. His soul had passed away.*

*The diamond ring he wore, was crushed and wet with
gore." Etc...etc...*

As the argument heated up, Vito became quite agitated, and
like a real tough guy started to throw his weight around. When
enlisting in the Corps, he had been very interested in seeing lots of
action, and consequently sought to join the famed Parachute Corps.
Instead, he was to suffer the humiliation of being assigned to the
lowly Quartermaster Corps, where his duties now included the
ignominious task of dispensing uniforms, skivvies and the like. He
took a lot of ribbing on this subject. But during his abusive tirade on
this night, he challenged Sgt. Baccus' authority after being told to
simmer down. The good Sgt. wisely backed off and avoided a direct
confrontation. However, Cpl. Alborn, another member of our group
stepped in, also ordering PFC Vito to settle down. Without hesitation,
the PFC went after the Cpl. and in a few seconds, the Cpl. was floored
by a rapid series of precisely delivered professional punches. And
then it was all over. No other challengers came forth when called
upon. A tense peace prevailed through the remainder of that night.
The next day, Alborn sported a pronounced mouse under one of his
eyes. Later, we were not surprised to learn that Vito was indeed a
professional boxer. His actions the previous night could have
ordinarily earned him a court martial, but scenes like this were not
uncommon with the troops stationed overseas, and so were typically
tolerated. Finding a true gentleman among overseas troops was just
not a reality. With the brass realizing that maybe he should be a
Paratrooper, Vito was quietly transferred out of our group.

11. ASSUMING DUTIES

Going back to the day of our arrival on Tutuila on December
15, 1942... I had been assigned to work on various Grumman-built
fighter planes and Douglas-built dive bombers. These planes were

parked in sheltered areas called revetments, which were camouflaged niches built along the jungle's edge, but still close to the runway. There were no hangars to accommodate our aircraft, with one exception, and that was to house huge balloons. These balloons were to be used early in the campaign as a Balloon Barrage defensive weapon, a rudimentary way of protecting the airfield and its buildings. Dozens of huge, blimp-like balloons were filled with hydrogen, and allowed to drift at altitudes of up to 5,000 feet over the airbase while tethered by steel cable to a winch-equipped truck on the ground. These cables were easily able to snag and destroy low flying enemy bombers. However, with the low probability of Samoa being bombed by aircraft at this time, the operation was scrapped.

On January 01, 1943, I was delighted to receive news of my promotion to Corporal (temporary, in the field). Unfortunately, on January 25, 1943, I once more came down with chronic tonsillitis. My weight had dropped from about 185 to 165 lbs., because I had no appetite, barely managing two meals a day. I should have had them removed eleven months prior while stationed in Quantico.

There was now no question that the tonsils had to come out immediately. On January 27, I was sent to the new 300 bed mobile hospital, located in the nearby inland village of Mapasaga. The simple operation took place the next day but with some complication. The first tonsil came out in one piece, but the other required painstaking and time-consuming carving out of many small pieces, all rotten. The gentle and grey haired Navy doctor claimed that in all his 35 years of medical practice, he had never before seen such a diseased tonsil. As the tedious procedure dragged on, the anesthesia started to wear off and I started feeling pain. After a feeble request by me for some relief, the doctor calmly replied: "I wish I could give you more morphine... but we're running low and will need all of it for the casualties soon coming in from Guadalcanal and the Solomons." Our mobile hospital had already been treating Marine casualties from these combat areas since last August, when that campaign was launched. My bed was not in the same ward as the combat casualties. During World War II, running low on morphine at hospitals in combat areas was not a rare occurrence. Many years later while being treated by an old retired Navy ENT, he told of occasionally being forced to treat Marine combat casualties in the field without the aid of any opiate painkillers.

Tensions seemed to abound throughout the airbase, especially in the chow line, and even in the hospital. One day I had to witness a serious fist fight between two ENT patients with their faces still stuffed with cotton from recent sinus surgeries. One grew so angry he started swinging wild haymakers at the other, so much so as to become completely exhausted and unable to raise his hands in his own defense. To his surprise, his opponent did not take advantage of the situation and simply backed off, leaving the aggressor to simmer down. After seven days, I was discharged from the hospital and put on light duty for another five days. I now found myself constantly hungry and eager for food, when previously I had little or no appetite. Unfortunately, our meals were made up of mostly dehydrated foods,… drab, poorly prepared and seldom appetizing.

After my brief hospital stay, I was not sent back to work on the flight lines, but instead given an entirely new assignment. At age 18, I certainly was no expert in aviation mechanics, as were all of my 40 comrades. However, I did possess the unique special qualification of being a bombsight and automatic pilot mechanic, the only one in this broad area of the South Pacific. This qualification was probably the prime reason for my being invited to come along on this special detail in the first place. But that work could not serve as a full time assignment, so it was now being augmented with one of overseeing the activities at the large aviation ammunition depot located in the adjacent jungle. This depot was meant to supply airbases within a 1,000 mile radius. I would be heading all work crews involved in handling shipments of ammo and bombs in and out of twelve magazine buildings scattered about in the jungle. It would also be my sole responsibility to keep records of all incoming and outgoing shipments, and to write up monthly records, which after signature by our Commanding Officer, Lt. Col. Benjamin Reisweber, would be sent directly to Naval Command Headquarters in Washington, DC. Our MCAF outfit was not subject to any Navy command in the Pacific, rather, we were to take orders directly from Washington. This assignment was probably the predominant factor for my recent promotion to Corporal. As a corporal I would be an NCO and have appropriate authority over work crews. My bombsight duties would still be given high priority, but only as the need arose.

Our small group soon grew to 140 personnel, mostly lower grade enlisted men to fill the ranks for carrying out the important everyday tasks of aircraft maintenance. This group also included our new Sargent Major, Ken Miller, assigned to oversee all enlisted men's activities. Also joining us was a new company clerk, Eugene Morrow. Even though I was never meant to be a book keeper, I managed to create my own crude system of keeping records. The Colonel signed all the reports I submitted without ever inspecting their contents. I was very pleased with having this complete trust afforded me. My big problem was of not having a regular work crew. Our MCAF's original compliment of men was now swelling, but they were all assigned to performing skilled work on damaged aircraft, and consequently could not be spared as permanent day laborers. When needed, I had to go out and round up unwilling volunteers from any available source. The bulk of these came from non-essential MAG 13 personnel, with a few men becoming almost regulars.

Among the almost regulars were three Navy enlisted men who somehow got left behind from an earlier campaign and then seemingly abandoned by the Navy. These orphaned sailors were cooperative and reliable workers. However, they sure were of differing personalities. First was Peterson, a young mid-western farm boy, very shy, who kept to himself. Next was Marty, a mature, older sailor, quiet and easygoing. Marty and I ordinarily sort of stuck together because we shared something in common: carriers of a rare blood type, AB+. We tried to be aware of each other's whereabouts, just in the case one of us came in need of a blood transfusion. The third sailor was Mitchell. Now, here was a character, a happy-go-lucky comedian with a great personality. You just had to like him. Mitchell became our special hero one day as a result of a confrontation with our much disliked Sgt. Major Miller. The argument was over some chicken-shit (meaningless) regulation that Miller insisted on enforcing. Well, it soon developed into a noisy fist fight and drew a small crowd. Much to our delight, Mitchell ended as the clear winner. Military regulations would have Mitchell court martialed, since the Sargent Major clearly outranked him. But, here we were dealing with two separate services of the military. Thankfully, the obnoxious but wise Miller, chose not to bring charges against Mitch, our hero of the day. Had the scuffle taken place between junior and senior NCO ranks within our own Marines, I'm sure charges would have been filed.

Among memorable characters skimmed from the ranks of MAG 13 personnel, was my good friend and namesake Leon Augustyn, a native of Peoria, Illinois. Leon was of Polish descent, as was I. He was a true comedian. He often talked about his close relationship with Muriel, his childhood sweetheart back home. He loved to rattle off poems that blended Polish with English lines. His never-ending chatter reeked of nonsense and trivia. Leon also looked the part of a comedian since he was short and stocky, and strutted about like a bantam rooster, and almost always sported a fat cigar sticking out of his mouth. He loved to refer to me as Kelly, the bum-bardier. In addition to fixing bombsights, I had also trained to be a bombardier. There also was Hashmark Hennessy. He had already earned his hashmark, the diagonal stripe worn on the lower sleeve for having served four years of duty in the Corps. Hashmark was an under-achiever, probably due to his being a victim of narcolepsy. He could fall asleep sitting or standing at almost any time of the day. While traveling on the road, we would often find him dozing off while standing upright and holding onto the crane structure of the bomb truck. He did, thankfully, manage to stay awake while handling ammunition and bombs. It seemed that whenever his body wasn't in motion, it brought on brief shuteyes.

The only regular from our own Air Facility group was Henry Simek, a native of Long Island, NY. Hank constantly and wistfully reminisced about returning home and marrying Peg, his childhood sweetheart. Hank had the odd habit of exhaling through his lit cigarette, inevitably producing a streaming cloud of hot ashes. Hank was also a bit of a pessimist and frequently dwelt on not ever making it back to the States alive. He seemed to be one of the first Marines to show signs of cracking up, or going Asiatic, as we were used to saying back then. During most of the day, he could be found just silently staring off into empty space.

Our group in the Air Facility did not sleep in the same area as did the men of MAG 13, but since I worked with them almost daily, we found time to relax together. One of those pleasantries was to go swimming in the lagoon at the end of the runway where it emptied into the sea. There were no nearby sandy beaches suitable for swimming. Most of the beachfront had protruding fields of lava deposits containing many vertical holes which were open to incoming crashing waves. These waves produced sharp, vertical sprays, producing an unfriendly environment. We called these sites blowholes.

Swimming in the area near the runway's end was unsafe also because of the presence of sharp and poisonous underwater coral outcroppings. In addition, treacherous currents were often encountered, obliging us to be on constant alert. One day, Leon was among a few of us busily exploring the sea bottom around these swirling waters. After a few minutes of horsing around, someone noticed that Leon had disappeared. We wasted no time combing the waters for him. He was quickly found, floundering about and in a confused state. We pulled him out in time and slowly brought him around. He remembered encountering and possibly being stung by what he described a large Portuguese Man-O'-War jellyfish. His comic mindset stepped in as he told us, "I remember thrashing around for a long time and not getting anywhere. Then, I just gave up and said …'Oh shit, the hell with it,'…and stopped trying." Typical Leon!

One other MAG 13 member was Zeke Gish, a refined sort of a chap who always showed a curiosity about new machinery and about all that was going on. We had just inherited a motorized crane with an adjustable boom, a real asset for readying bombs for transport. Previously, we had to use a hand cranked claw hanging off an iron I-beam that was welded to the bed of an open bed truck. I had not had a chance to get checked out on the complex controls of the new piece of machinery. One day, I decided to sit in the driver's seat and test each control handle, but kept getting only erratic and jerking movements from all the moving parts. Finally, I asked Zeke to grab hold of the claw, dangling just above the ground. He did so, but then found himself jerked off the ground as I applied the first control that seemed appropriate. He yelled at me to let him down, but my efforts resulted in his being jerked up higher and higher. In less than a minute, a very irate Zeke was hanging on for dear life, about 15 feet above the ground. Then the vindictive expletives started to pour out of Zeke's mouth, all directed at me. He wanted to kill me. I was at a loss for what to try next. Finally, I did find the right buttons and slowly brought him down. As soon as his feet hit the ground, like a wounded bull, he came charging right at me. I steeled, anticipating a flurry of punches, but all that ensued was some sputtering and cursing, and then he finally simmered down. Zeke was smaller in stature than me, perhaps tempering his anger. I apologized profusely, and he, as a true gentleman, accepted.

There were other memorable characters worthy of mention. Some were from our MCAF, while others were with MAG 13. From Air Facility, was Mel Belcher. Mel was a lady's man, who wasted no time in taking advantage of the friendliness of the native girls. Mel had a very annoying habit of butting into any conversation to put in his two cents. He was always ready to deliver a story or an experience that he was certain would be of interest to all of us. After a while, these interruptions got to us and we decided something had to be done to end them. Our solution was simple: wait until just before he was about to jump into an ongoing conversation with his contribution, then immediately have everyone in the group jump in together, repeating a chorus of: "Tell us about it, Mel; aw c'mon, tell us about it." This ploy eventually got to him, and after a few repetitions of this scene, he came back at us, bellowing "F--- you guys, I ain't never gonna to tell you nuthin." We really hurt his feelings, but the treatment worked and he stopped butting in, at least within our group. Another nameless character was a totally unsavory one who turned up in the evening hours always totally inebriated. When asked to leave the fale by our Sgt. Baccus, he would slur back some obscenity, always followed by incorrectly addressing the sergeant as Sgt. "Baxter." After being corrected again, he would exit with a crude, final farewell to Sgt. "Baxley."

Our company clerk, Eugene Morrow, was a New Yorker and not very popular - one certainly bearing no resemblance to Radar O'Reilly, the lovable company clerk in the TV M*A*S*H series. Morrow was a diehard pessimist. Conversations with him typically were dominated by a litany of personal complaints. He played payday poker with us on a regular basis, and always bellyached with details of how much money he was losing, when he really seldom did actually lose. His way of playing was to quit soon after getting a few winning hands, and then send his money home. He always claimed to be losing, although he invariably had more money in hand when he quit than when he started. This routine undoubtedly was laudable with his family back home, but not with his family of troops on this island.

Another character whom all in MAG 13 found friendly was Snuffy Smith. Snuffy was a sea shell aficionado. He spent almost all his spare time combing the adjacent beaches for colorful seashells. It didn't take long for him to acquire a bad case of tropical fungus. He wound up in the mobile hospital with an advanced case which eventually spread internally. When Snuffy started losing weight at an alarming rate, the medical staff realized that he would not survive unless he was removed from the tropics and sent back to the USA for treatment. How to get him back to the States alive was a problem. He might not survive a long two week sea voyage, but to fly for long hours at high altitudes was considered even riskier. When his weight dropped to 90 pounds, it was decided to ship him by sea. In later years, through the Navy scuttlebutt, we learned that he made it back to the States and did fully recover. All of us who spent more than a few months in the tropics, picked up recurring fungus infections on our feet and our groin, and often still find them virtually impossible to permanently get rid of.

There was also Sgt. Macko, a slightly older chap who made the Corps his home. He was a bit on the sad side. He had no family back home and this was obvious on Mail Call day, typically every three weeks when the mail was flown in from Hawaii and distributed among the troops as they lined up for dinner chow. This affair always brought on lots of hooting and joyful hollering as the eager troops snapped up the letters and packages from home. However, no mail ever came for Macko. The Marine Corps was his only family. This proved even sadder at Christmas time as packages arrived from loving families back home. Lastly, Macko always kept a hat on his head, not a typical habit for anyone in this tropical environment. The reason for this was that he was a bit self-conscious about being rather bald, a rarity for troops of young age.

One occupant of a neighboring fale did find a satisfying way of mitigating his loneliness. He used his upper bunk as an altar, and almost daily managed to solitarily conduct a Catholic religious mass. In his youth, he had been an altar boy. One day, I experienced a happy occasion as I was about to enter the post exchange, and heard a voice call out: "Hey, Walt!" It turned out to be a classmate from my high school graduation class. His name was Leo Savitsky. Having served his time on the front lines, he now had the good fortune of being in the process of shipping back to the States. He gladly agreed to convey a message to my family back home and to assure them I was in good health and in no danger.

12. THE TRAGIC CELEBRATION

In the Spring of 1943, MAG-13 found a few troops arriving to replace those being released for return to the States, those who had been among the first to be stationed at the airbase early in 1942. Upon receiving this welcome word, one of these recipients from MAG 13's Motor Pool, felt the occasion called for a grand celebration. His tour of overseas duty was over. However, there was no source of beer or booze for the enlisted men stationed on this, or any other island. Navy regulations forbade enlisted men having any alcoholic beverages on base. The Navy eased this rule on two past occasions with the shipment a few thousand cases of beer, which were distributed to all enlisted men on the island,... two (warm) bottles to each Marine. Those who did not drink had no trouble finding eager recipients for their unwanted share.

The alcohol shortage problem did not exist for the officers. Booze was available to them at all times. Enlisted men had to find some other source, and they tried to do so with the use of homemade stills, a practice commonly found in many overseas military camps. That night a wild night party ensued in the Motor Pool section. However, the next morning, the party's participants were understandably horrified upon learning that last night's guest of honor was found dead in his sack. Except for harboring very bad hangovers, none of the rest of them felt very sick. However, around noon, word came from the medical staff announcing the cause of death to be from alcohol poisoning, and strongly directed all of the party drinkers to turn themselves in to the mobile hospital and have their stomachs pumped, then stay for observation. The situation at the time did not seem that dire, since the medical staff was not expecting any additional fatalities or afflictions, except for one individual who had reportedly drank a lot of home-brew. This guy was in his 40s and reported to be an old rummy, who in the past, drank any intoxicating concoction he could get his hands on, including ordinary anti-freeze. However, the med staff projected that even he might suffer only some degree of blindness.

Even though I didn't have any real close friends in the Motor Pool, I accompanied a bunch of non-party participants to a visit to the mobile hospital that evening. All the sick men, and there seemed to be a lot of them, were in beds, writhing in discomfort and occasionally throwing up. Still, there seemed little concern about the anticipated outcome of the unfolding scenario. In fact, some observers made light of the situation by starting a dime pool, betting to see which sick man would throw up next. That was the scene when visiting hours expired and we visitors were told to leave. At about midnight, the medical staff got the shock of their life as the sick men rapidly began dying. By dawn the next day, the count revealed that eighteen hearty and healthy young Marines had perished. One, whom I casually knew, was an athlete and former all American football star in civilian life, who had refrained from drinking anything alcoholic in his entire adult life, but had been coaxed at the party into downing a mere half a shot of the concoction. On the other hand, the old rummy who was expected to suffer some degree of blindness, survived without any bad effects.

The entire air base went into shock. Further investigation revealed the concoction to be almost pure methanol, a known poison for which there was no known antidote. The alcohol in social drinking is primarily ethyl alcohol. Of course the brass immediately responded with a directive ordering a clean sweep of the base, searching out and confiscating any homemade stills that were producing alcohol. It was no secret that simple alcohol stills had generally existed around isolated overseas military bases. Their most popular product, known as "Raisin Jack," was made mostly from ordinary fruits. This drink always gave you a hangover when consumed in any quantity, but was never considered toxic. Most confiscated stills were very simple, but a few stood out as rather sophisticated. Those particular ones were built by our resident Navy Construction Battalion (CBs) who were stationed about the islands and were responsible for building runways, buildings, bridges, etc. These were almost all elderly journeymen, not trained for combat. They knew how to build just about anything. The still that produced the poison methanol turned out to be a small, crude one, and had used ordinary shellac as a base in the distillation process. The owners and operators of that still were two young Marine privates, 18 and 21 years of age. They were totally unaware of the deadly difference between safe ethanol, and poisonous methanol.

This terrible tragedy now posed a perplexing problem for the staff officers who were assigned the unenviable task of having to send this devastating news back home to the families of the deceased. What could one possibly say to them? Certainly not that their loved ones had perished in such an ignominious manor. Family at home seemed always to ask the same questions when given the bad news of one of their loved ones in uniform as having perished overseas. "How did he die?" "Was he alone?" "Did he suffer much?" "What were his last words?" It would be relatively easy to say that he died a hero in the defense of his country, or for a noble cause. In contrast however, the sad event that happened to these 18 Marines on the island of Samoa was truly tragic, because these Marines died for absolutely no cause. No, the only acceptable message would simply be: "He died in the line of duty."

This sort of sad situation would be repeated many times as the war dragged on. Many troops had accidently been shot and killed along battle lines by their own comrades, better referred to as friendly fire. Or more so, by errors and oversights committed by the military commanders, such as happened late in the war in the case when the Navy cruiser, the Indianapolis, was sunk by a Japanese sub as it sailed unescorted on a long journey between two outlying sea bases. Navy monitors should have been periodically checking its safe passage along the trip, but they neglected to do so, and when the ship failed to arrive at its destination, nobody was aware of it. Of the entire crew of approximately 1,200 men aboard, 300 went down with the ship. The remaining 900 abandoned ship, and spent five harrowing days in the shark-infested ocean. Of these, only 316 managed to survive and be rescued. The ship's radio SOS had not been picked up, because no one was listening to the right frequency. During those five days, approximately 600 sailors were lost to drowning or relentless shark attacks, all because no one had been checking on the ship's whereabouts.

In MAG 13, the two responsible Marines were promptly arrested and awaited trial. Judicial courts in the field rarely existed. A call was sent to the Navy legal department in the States to send down a Judge Advocate to conduct court in the field. This took a few months. This man had the rank of Captain and was also given the additional duty as the officer-in-charge of MAG 13's ordnance group.

When he arrived, it was obvious to us that he was not a career officer, but more a so-called 90-day wonder, one who entered the Navy with a commission, and then attended a crash course in Navy leadership. Since I already had been mixing in with the two MAG 13 senior ordnance NCOs, it now required my spending some time in the Captain's presence. He was not in great physical shape, being somewhat overweight. He hailed from Texas and carried about him the typical southern good ole boy demeanor. With regard to conducting the affairs within the Ordnance department, his announcement to the two NCOs was "You boys just go right along with what you've been doin' and don't let me interfere." This put everyone around at ease. Then, over the coming weeks, he delved into details of the coming trial of the two Marines under arrest. He regaled on his experiences of working in a police department in a large Texas city, bragging how he and his staff got some suspects (especially minorities) to talk. He eagerly went into ghoulish details, like pulling out fingernails and setting hair on fire. We listened in shock. Obviously, he was enjoying the moment. Then he turned the conversation to the two Marines he was to prosecute and calmly announced that he intended to seek a conviction of first degree murder. Now, this dumbfounded us. Everyone on the airbase believed the two young Marines intended to make simple drinking alcohol and honestly meant no harm to anyone.

After a few weeks passed, the Captain pulled another shocker as he haughtily announced to his two NCOs (and me): "Boys, the party's over, this (Ordnance) department is now going to be run my way!" By golly he's probably going to run things just like he did in Texas. Again, we were dumbfounded! The department had been running very smoothly so far. This stern announcement caught us all by complete surprise. Fortunately for me, I didn't have to take orders from this guy, since I was not a member of MAG-13. However, as the weeks rolled by, I had to watch and sympathize with the two senior NCOs.

The trial eventually did take place and the accused privates were ultimately convicted of a lesser charge, that of second degree murder. They then received their sentence: "to serve an indeterminate time in the Naval prison at Ft. Leavenworth, Kansas," basically a life sentence. Many months later, as we were all being shipped back to the

States, I served as one of the brig sentries aboard ship, in the capacity of a 24 hour guard over these two prisoners. These poor guys were really remorseful, and seemed like real nice guys. Much later while Stateside, we were happy to learn through scuttlebutt, that the two had their sentences temporarily suspended with the stipulation that they return to the front lines of the battlefront and stay there until the war ended, no matter how long it lasted. No reference was made to a possible commutation of their sentences, although in our minds, that remained a possibility. The misery-causing Captain had already been called back for duty in the States. None of us at the air base felt sad to have this poor excuse for an officer depart from our lives.

13. A NEW TROPICAL DISEASE

With the island now swelling with new Marines, a considerable influx of casualties suddenly began flowing into our sick bay mobile hospital. Prior to this, except for the ever present fungus infections, the troops felt they were living on a tropical paradise. Slowly, but surely, we watched as a new sickness slowly invaded our ranks. Symptoms were much like those of malaria: aches, high fever and extreme fatigue, resulting in a complete inability to carry out one's daily tasks. The medical staff wasn't sure how the disease was being transmitted, and originally classified it as being one due to the tropical climate. You got it by just being in this hot and humid atmosphere. It was finally diagnosed as filariasis, and speculated that it was spread by mosquitoes belonging to the same family as that of the malaria carrying mosquitoes. This was a mystery because American Samoa had been declared a malaria-free island. Even more perplexing was the fact that there had never been any previous outbreaks of filariasis among servicemen in the Pago Pago harbor area, even though a small contingent of American servicemen had been stationed there since the year 1900.

Obviously, the recent heavy influx of troops acted as a wildfire mechanism for spreading the disease. The medical brass had to take great pains in keeping this tropical disease from being further spread among the islands. Some strict rules had to be followed. All planes, upon arrival from nearby island air bases were forced to have their occupants sit inside the closed planes for ten minutes while an aerosol bomb was released inside the plane's cabin with the intent to kill all insects, especially mosquitoes. The natives called the disease mumu. The troops called it elephantitis, because it occasionally caused the development of inordinate swelling of certain lymph glands. Among a few natives, having lived there all their lives, it could cause one of their legs to swell to several times its normal diameter, suggesting that of an elephant's leg.

Servicemen afflicted would be totally knocked out of commission and required to undergo complete bed rest. There was no cure at that time. To help stem the rapid spreading of the disease, we were told to wear as much clothing as could be tolerated, and to stay away from native villages, especially at night. However, some troops continued to make the choice of frequently visiting these villages at night in pursuit of favors from the accommodating native women. Gradually, the disease spread to other nearby islands, anywhere there happened to be a recent high influx of non-natives. Rumors also circulated that the disease could very likely leave an afflicted man sterile. Dreams of raising a family upon return to the States suddenly looked bleak. Morale among us plummeted. At the air base, we started losing many men from MCAF, as well as from those in MAG 13, but more telling was the loss among the thousands of troops spread throughout remote parts of the island, and especially those stationed in special camps deep in the jungle undergoing special training, then subsequently being sent into combat on other islands.

Unlike treatments for malaria, taking quinine would not prevent contracting filariasis. You were put into the hospital, got complete bed rest for a period of a few weeks until your strength returned, and were then simply sent back to duty, sometimes back to the front lines. A few afflicted troops actually went through this cycle more than once. After a long and stressful period of indecision on the medical front, the Navy finally took strong action and directed that all afflicted personnel be sent to the States for treatment immediately upon first detection of the disease. Scuttlebutt also had it that the high Navy brass, after reviewing how the situation had been mishandled, considered court martial for the hospital's senior medical staff. The considered cure at this time was to send the afflicted troops to an entirely different climate, cold and dry, like some winter resort in the Rocky Mountains area. However, it was later learned that they all wound up at Marine barracks at Klammath Falls, OR, where after the war, records show that about 3,000 men underwent treatment, and subsequently were cured using a newly developed serum.

In my immediate group, it seemed that every man who had turned himself in to sick bay with the tell-tale symptoms of fatigue and swollen red lumps on his arm or armpit would return with a loud announcement: "I'm going home, I'm going home!" It then became apparent to a few enterprising young Marines, that all of us were possibly carrying the disease. Some men followed a daily process of vigorously rubbing a same spot on their arm in hopes of raising a distinct red welt. Soon after a welt appeared, they hustled over to sick bay, falsely complaining of fatigue and such, and to everyone's surprise, a blood test showed that they were carrying the filariasis bug. Most received orders to be immediately shipped back to the States for treatment. Soon after, the Navy announced that the tour of duty in this area (that length of time necessary before earning the right to return to the States) was being reduced from 18 to 12 months.

Those of us who stayed behind were now convinced that almost every Marine who had been on the island for a few months was now carrying the disease, even if he wasn't showing the usual symptoms. Most of us naively clung to the "Not me" syndrome. In my case, I felt protected, since I was one of three men carrying a rare blood type, none of whom showed any signs of the disease. Also, since we knew for certain that the disease was a mosquito borne one, I made it a point to wear long sleeve shirts and long pants at all times, especially when working in the jungle among the ammo magazine buildings. In addition, I completely refrained from frequenting native villages, especially at night. In the end, about half of our group's specialists in MCAF were surveyed (meaning, sent back to the States as useless).

By late spring of 1943, the island's military population was significantly dropping. As a consequence of the large influx of Marines into Samoa, culminating in the rapid spread of filariasis to other parts of the Pacific, it was decided to discontinue having Samoa serve as this area's primary hub for any future jungle training. Of much more significance to us at MCAF was that Navy Headquarters in DC decided to scrap their lofty plan of having our special detail set up an aircraft overhaul base close to enemy lines. But now what happens to us in MCAF? Rather than splitting us up and transferring us to different airbases in the area, the same high Navy brass decided that we should stay here as a Headquarters Squadron (without planes). We would continue to run this airbase and large ammunition depot as best we could, while maintaining our personnel strength at about 150.

14. PREPARING FOR THE BIG PUSH

Having achieved a marginal naval battle victory in the Coral Sea in May of 1942, and the more recent clear cut victory at Midway in June of 1942, the Navy landed the 1st Division Marines on Guadalcanal in the Solomon Island Group on August 07, 1942. The land and sea battle see-sawed for a while, such that a withdrawal was contemplated. A few weeks later in August, in order to draw Japanese attention away from the Solomons, the Navy conducted a diversionary hit-and-run landborne raid on Makin Island, located in the northern tier of the North Central Pacific Gilbert Island chain. Later, on October 02, the US Navy boldly moved unchallenged into the Ellice Islands, approximately halfway between Samoa and the Japanese stronghold of Tarawa in the Gilberts. The 5th Marine Defense Battalion moved in to occupy the three main islands of Funafuti, Nanomea and Nukufetau. Navy Seabees hurriedly built an airstrip on the main island of Funafuti with fighter planes from MAG 13 moving in immediately after. The Samoan area Commanding Officer, Major General Price made the first plane landing there 30 days later. However, the island received no further planes for air defenses until late January, 1943. Fighter planes were desperately needed for the Guadalcanal campaign, and so were drawn from the MAG 13 squadrons stationed in the air defense area of Samoa such that very few of them were left to defend Samoa, Upolu and Wallis.

In April of 1943, Seventh Army Air Corps four-engine B-24s were flown into Funafuti and soon found themselves trading air raids with Japanese bombers from Tarawa, 700 miles to the north. To avoid detection, the Japanese bombers would occasionally approach Funafuti at a high altitude, and while still many miles away, cut their engines and slowly and silently glide down over the airfield before releasing their bombs. One of their raids was particularly destructive, when on a moonlit night, two B-24s on the ground were destroyed, and several others were damaged. Also, a native church, which had just been jammed with natives seeking shelter from the raid, was blown to bits. Fortunately, just minutes before, a Marine guard under orders, had by gunpoint, forced all the natives to abandon the church and safely disperse into the adjoining coconut tree area.

The actual effectiveness of our B-24 bombers raids was highly doubtful. Scuttlebutt reaching us in Samoa, and probably exaggerated, had it that during the many months of B-24 raids, not a single bomb had found its mark on targets on the island of Tarawa. Further, we lost more than a few bombers, but not to enemy fire. It was said that the range of the bombers was being put to the test, and that some bombers couldn't quite make it all the way back to Funafuti, or got lost, resulting in a frantic scramble to land, with some having to ditch their planes almost within sight of the island. Also, in general, the Japanese air raids were found to be similarly ineffective. Operations on the island must have been somewhat chaotic given how small the island was and with so many big bombers based there. It was said that at any particular time of the day, no bombers were to be found on land, meaning some were always in the air, either going or returning from air raids on Tarawa. The Marine fighter planes from MAG 13 did on two occasions down enemy bombers over Funafuti. Later that year, B-24s started operations from Nanomea and eventually from Nukufetau, hence, from all three islands in the Ellice group.

Throughout the summer of 1943, work routines around the twelve ammunition magazines at Tutuila became routine. I spent part of my time in and around the complex of offices spread around the east side of the airbase toward the harbor at Pago Pago. We still had our original seasoned warrant officers running operations at the air base. However, one day a rookie was added to the ranks. He surely did not fit the mold of his fellow officers. Lt. Haskins was only 19 or 20 years old and obviously came in to the Corps as a 90-day wonder. His title was that of the Bomb Disposal Officer. Unlike the disgusting Captain in MAG-13, this guy was so naïve, and at times, comical looking, such that he took a steady stream of kidding from his aged fellow officers. When talking about him when he wasn't present, he was simply referred to as Bomb Disposal. Likewise, when these senior officers spoke of me when I was not in their presence, the title they afforded me was a simple "Bombsight."

It was a rather strange situation to be very young and inexperienced in life to be periodically immersed in a pool of very experienced and life-savvy old timers. They sure conducted themselves differently than the average G.I. Joe did in his barracks, or in our case, our fales. They had their fun in different ways, but in the final analysis, their antics and horsing around probably wasn't that much different than what went on among the enlisted men. I was somewhat shocked one day when hearing them refer to our Commanding Officer, Lt Col Benjamin Reisweber, as "Screaming Bennie." It turns out that when the Colonel would on occasion, get excited over some matter, the pitch of his voice would rise to the point that it sounded very much like he was screaming. I must say that I was always treated with respect by all the officers, young and old, and never remember being put down or reprimanded, even though I may have deserved it.

Consolidated PBY-5A Catalina Patrol Bomber

15. WORKING ON PBYs – A TRIP TO AUSTRALIA?

Going back to May of 1943, I made my first recorded flight in a PBY, finally assuming some responsibility in working with its Norden Bombsight, and more often, its automatic pilot system. I had previously made local inflight repairs as early as January, but these were never reported in writing. The PBY was a heavy amphibious twin engine patrol bomber, but its primary function in this area was in performing sea-air rescues. MAG-13 had two of them stationed at Tutuila. These planes historically happened to be the very first PBYs assigned to Marine Corps Aviation. These first two planes also experienced much use in transporting personnel and equipment between islands. These flights often required long times in the air, since distances between islands were typically many hundreds of miles. The large surface area on the plane's rudder required much physical effort by the pilot, in keeping the plane on course. Even though this control was primarily assisted by hydraulic power, they still required constant exertion by the pilot on the foot pedals controlling the rudder position. Some flights took as much as five hours in the air. Without the assist of the autopilot, the pilot could find himself completely exhausted upon reaching his destination. On one occasion, a pilot had to be physically assisted out of the cockpit and out of the plane after one of these flights. Having the autopilot take over flying the plane rendered this task relatively easy. The pilots liked to count on having their autopilot in tip top working order, especially when embarking on long flights.

Throughout that summer, demand for my autopilot expertise became more and more frequent. The autopilot malfunction could seldom be checked or repaired on the ground. The system was an electronic sophistication that required a delicate touch on a sprawling array of control knobs mounted on the pilot's overhead panel. The popular complaint, or squawk, by the pilot was that the plane was wandering all over the sky, that is, yawing back and forth. My diagnosis of the problem frequently turned out to be cockpit trouble. That meant the pilot didn't really know what he was doing as he tried setting up the controls. These electronic controls called for a patient and delicate touch, and usually required taking the plane up for an actual test flight. Thus, I eventually became a temporary crew member.

On occasion, the problem would require opening up the complex mechanical devices and getting inside to do some cleanup and mechanical adjustments. There was the extreme condition where salt water had made its way into the gyroscope housings which contained the delicate mechanics of the system. The PBY was an amphibious plane, meaning it was built to land on water as well as on land. Salt water landings were usually very rough, especially when taking place on the open sea with spray getting into the bombardier's compartment in the nose of the fuselage. Salt water intrusion could cause extensive corrosion and a dilemma, especially when it accessed delicate and precisely manufactured ball bearings used in and around the gyroscope mechanisms. Incredibly, I somehow managed to patch up these problems, barely keeping the systems operative. I managed all this without having access to any maintenance manuals or any special tools with which to work, and most importantly, no spare parts. Finally, I found it necessary to inform the brass that the situation was now becoming hopeless, that I must have an operator's manual, tools, and above all, spare parts. This plea was summarily heeded and followed by good news. A supply of these tools, parts and manuals was readily available at a supply base in Sydney, Australia. Further, I was being authorized to catch a flight there and pick up everything I needed. I must be dreaming...this was too good to be true!

Getting off this island to visit any civilized city was just too much to hope for. Up to this time, no enlisted man from MCAF had managed to pay a visit to any other neighboring island. On two separate occasions, I did get to fly to neighboring Upolu when autopilots needed fixing. In contrast to Tutuila, the entire island of Upolu was comparatively civilized, whereas in American Samoa over the many years, only the harbor area had been developed. A contingent of MAG-13 was stationed in Upolu as well as elements of defense units from the Seventh Marine Regiment. These troops, as well as pilots stationed there all considered Upolu to be a paradise compared to Tutuila. Upolu had much flat ground. On my first visit there, while on the ground, the flight crew of two and myself, traveled down the road from the airstrip at Faleole to the capital city of Apia. Along the way, we passed several unique small villages and some farms with cattle grazing in the fields.

We stopped at a small roadside restaurant and chowed down a batch of hamburgers! The natives here were much more civilized than those found in the outlying villages in Tutuila. Girls wore full length flowered skirts, compared to plain lava lavas worn on Tutuila. They also spoke better English. The young native waitress assigned to our table bubbled with enthusiasm as she took our orders and served us. As she giggled, she repeatedly injected a phrase in native Upolan language, one which we did not understand. It went "Kio oi, Melingi." When curiosity finally got the best of us, we called the maître d' over to our table. She was a mature and stately looking woman. She very apologetically offered the following explanation: "That expression means the same thing as 'Hai Kai, Melingi' in American Samoan." She further explained that the children pick up the expression of Hai Kai, or Kia Oi, when they are very young and it stays with them. Also, it is only meant as a positive and friendly greeting. The language differed between both islands. Upolu had been taken over from the German empire at the end of WW I, and was put under the mandate of the New Zealand government, as part of the British Empire. Early in history, Christian missionaries visited and helped develop all British held islands in this area of the Pacific.

Looking forward to a trip to Sydney, Australia, was really something to get excited about. Sydney was reported to be the best R&R city in the entire Pacific, including Hawaii. Its inhabitants treated all American servicemen as real heroes. This was due in part to the almost complete absence of Australian servicemen, who paradoxically had been all sent to fight on the European battlefront much before the Japanese initiated the war in the Pacific. I was now all set to catch that flight to Sydney the next morning. All the officers at MCAF's command post, as well as the bunkmates in my fale were left green with envy, but nevertheless extended their sincere congratulations on my good fortune.

However, the next morning brought crushing news. My trip was off! Someone else had been designated to pick up those tools and spare parts. It wasn't me! It had to be a seasoned bombsight/autopilot mechanic who would have the knowledge of choosing the right assortment of tools and parts. However, I was the only bombsight/ autopilot mechanic in this entire area of the South Pacific, right?! This was a fact and everybody knew it. Remember, it was I who occasionally had to leave my work post at the ammunition depot and go along on a flight that needed having its autopilot fixed, since there was nobody else qualified to do it. Finally, the cat came out of the bag. Out steps a First Lt. Bunny Paulis, a member of MAG-13, a supposedly qualified bombsight mechanic. Where did he come from? Why didn't he come forth when there was such a strong need for an autopilot mechanic? No answers to these queries followed. I met the man that day and I was not impressed. He was short in stature and pudgy, and strange as it seems, he wore sneakers. He in no way exemplified a typical career Marine Corps officer, but probably was a college graduate and entered the service as another 90-day wonder. He managed a weak apology accompanied by the classic shit eating grin. That was it! Tough shit, pal, Lt. Bunny Paulis outranked this hapless Corporal. Sorry, pal. And so, Lt. Paulis did make this mission to Sydney and bring back all the detailed stuff I requested. But afterwards he never did lend a hand in fixing any autopilots. In fact I never ran across him at any later date. I can only deduce that he at one time did attend Norden Bombsight School or perhaps as a crash course, but afterwards, never touched a bombsight in use. Obviously, he didn't wish any further involvement.

I felt sure that this fiasco made the officers in MCAF feel bad about being powerless in preventing this miscarriage of justice. On September 13, 1943, my hurt feelings were somewhat assuaged upon being informed that I was to be promoted to Sargent. In the middle of the month? Unheard of! This was not the norm, but more likely a move to appease my hurt feelings. My last promotion to the rank of Corporal took place almost nine months earlier, so it was about time anyway. It took place a week before my 19th birthday. Also, keep in mind that I still worked under a great group of MCAF officers. I really did not have it so bad, after all.

16. MY NEW QUARTERS

In August of 1943, Brigadier General Harold D. Campbell, the air commander for this of the area of the Pacific, moved his headquarters from MCAS at Ewa in Hawaii, to Tutuila. This had to be a significant move by our military, in setting a springboard for an offensive in the North Pacific. Then in October of 1943, he was replaced by Brigadier General Lewis G. Merritt, who brought along with him four squadrons of a new air wing, MAG-31. These squadrons were spread among our airbases on Tutuila, Upolu, Wallis and Funafuti. Air activities increased dramatically, requiring seemingly endless shipments of bombs and ammo from my magazines. Housing all this new air personnel became a problem. I was moved out of my comfortable fale, and set up to live in a shack in the jungle, in the middle of a spread of the twelve ammunition magazines. This move would also ease the task of fulfilling the more frequent outgoing ammo shipments. To my surprise, I was not to be alone. Thankfully, I would have company. My companions were already known to me. They were the two senior NCOs; the same ones discussed in my review of the alcohol poisoning tragedy.

We were now several road miles from the airbase. Fortunately, we had a Jeep at our disposal. Also, we did have electricity specially lined in for us. The shortcomings were that of the long distance to the latrine and the highly desirable showers, both now several miles away. Additionally, I missed the nightly card games and the camaraderie of my regular fale buddies, who were all more or less of my rank and my age. However, these mature two senior NCOs were really nice guys. We shared tasks and activities around the magazines, and worked well together. It was just that we had very little in common. They were much older and also outranked me. Consequently, there was very little two way conversation. Listening in on their conversations was unavoidable. I was about to lead a relatively solitary life for the foreseeable future.

There was a brief period where Dutch Holland, one of the two senior NCOs became absent for a few days. When he reappeared, he had a wild story to tell. In an operating aircraft group such as MAG-13, an occasional aviation ordnance duty existed which required the towing of aerial targets to be used in aerial gunnery for the group's fighter plane pilots. This task used an ungamely-looking, single engine, double winged amphibious plane, the Grumman J2F, also known as the "Duck." Its single, under-belly pontoon looked bigger than its entire fuselage. However, it proved to be a very versatile plane. Its fuselage had a downstairs compartment which was used to stow rescued pilots from downed planes, as well as for mail delivery, which occurred about every two weeks. It handily stowed an aerial tow target mechanism for use by pilots in gunnery practice. This task was not a comfortable one and no one relished being the operator. This type of small plane usually experienced a rather bumpy flight. The previously assigned MAG-13 operator was Sgt. Macko. During his last outing, he had become violently air sick and afterwards begged out of any future assignment.

A few days later, it fell upon Sgt. Holland's shoulders to take over the run. Since MAG-13 had fighter planes deployed on both

Tutuila and Upolu, the run would take place in the vicinity of both islands, but far enough to the west so as to not interfere with flight paths over the two airbases. After the aerial gunnery practice was successfully completed with Dutch at the operator's post, the Duck started to head for home, a distance of less than 100 miles. However, a large tropical storm suddenly erupted, fully blocking their return paths to either Tutuila or Upolu. The Duck did not have the long range capability of reaching the nearest clear weather island of Wallis, some 300 miles away. However, they found themselves only a few miles offshore of Savaii, the biggest island of the Samoa chain. Savaii was sparsely populated, did not have a deep seaport or an airfield. Only a small military presence was kept there. The pilot made the decision to land the Duck just offshore of what looked like a big native village. It was now getting late and the thought of having to spend the night here did not look very enticing.

Tutuila and Upolu were relatively developed and civilized, but Savaii remained a mystery to us Marines. I sat in wonder as Dutch went on and told us what transpired that evening. Dutch and his pilot were given a warm welcome at the shoreline by a fleet of outrigger canoes, and then promptly whisked to the village and its elders. These people probably never had the opportunity of meeting someone who had just dropped in from the sky. There, they were given the royal treatment. A big feast was quickly organized. Dutch and his pilot were each assigned two natives, one to fan the guest and the other to fan his food. There followed a lengthy entertainment of dancing. When it finally came time to hit the sack, the native chief called together his daughters and asked Dutch to choose one of them with whom he wished to sleep. Dutch gracefully tried to decline the generous offer, but got nowhere. He did manage to survive the night and fly back to regular duty early the next day.

At the jungle camp there was one other recurring topic that managed to garner my attention. That topic was censorship. Censorship was a fact of life out here in the battlefield regions, especially since the safety of every troop stationed among these islands and of ship movements at sea could be compromised by loose tongues, or in carelessly letters written home. Photo taking was strictly prohibited. All letters being sent home had to first be censored by the hand of a selected commissioned officer. Writers were never allowed to even hint as to our island's location. My sweetheart, as well as my folks at home had been told only that I was stationed on an island somewhere in the South Pacific. Censoring personal letters to home could be a daunting and unappealing task for any officer assigned to it, so it was not unusual for that task to be passed down to a senior NCO under his charge. Dutch and Ben were unfortunate to be chosen by their senior officer, MAG-13's obnoxious 90-day wonder Captain from Texas. They also received a free hand for this task and, being very mature, proved to be well suited for its execution. I was occasionally present when one of them read out a selected passage from some enlisted man's letter to home. These passages were invariably sensitive, and I always felt somewhat embarrassed when having to listen to them. I didn't have much of a choice, except to excuse myself and step outside.

There was really no place to go in the evening. At the main base, movies were infrequent and hardly worth attending. No post exchange. About the only available entertainment was to be with friends, play cards, and have a good bull session. On one particular night, Dutch and Ben decided to take the Jeep and spend the evening in town. I was now alone, which in itself should not have been a big deal. But the weather changed all that. A sudden storm appeared, and I assumed it was the usual evening thunderstorm. As the hours passed however, the winds grew stronger and stronger. When I started to hear trees crashing down regularly, I realized that a cyclone was now paying the islands a visit. The wind noise was hardly bearable, but more so was the increasing frequency of crashing trees. Each time I heard the sound of one coming down, I would dive under the table for shelter. I was rapidly becoming paranoid about staying there any longer by myself. Finally, I snapped. I panicked! I decided to get the hell out of there... right then! I took off in the total darkness down the Jeep trail, heading for the safety and companionship of the airbase. As I got nearer the base, I became more desperate and decided to shortcut through the jungle. I didn't look for pathways, but just plowed ahead. When I emerged at the jungle's edge, I saw exposed airbase buildings being torn apart and witnessed a large metal roof being ripped off a building and blown away, and the wind really howling. Seeing I was no longer alone, I once more felt safe. In reflecting back on being taken over by panic, I realized that this temporary state of mind had accomplished nothing. I had lost all sense of reasoning as I panicked, and all I had to show for it was a slew of arm and body scratches. It would have been much safer for me to stick it out in the jungle. And ever since, I have remained resolute to never again allow myself to become a victim of panic.

Another problem surfacing in December more frequently was having to leave my work post at the ammo magazines to attend to my other responsibility, that of fixing PBYs' autopilots. In addition, I should have been regularly receiving compensation for hazardous flight pay, a reward of an additional 50% to one's base pay. I was being denied this extra money because of the simple fact that MCAF had no planes of its own and thereby none of its members were entitled to hazard pay. In November of 1943, several pleas had been made by my immediate superior officer, Lt. Henry Camper, to see that I start getting this compensation through MAG-13, whose ranks had many men receiving this flight pay compensation. These pleas continued to fall on deaf ears. Lt. Camper was a patient man, but one day he called me in and told me straight out: "Kelly, I want you to stop flying until they start paying you." I felt terrible about this sort of confrontation, especially this being wartime, perhaps making me look a bit insubordinate. I shuddered at the thought of my possibly becoming a problem to my immediate superior officers.

But this move did prompt some real action. At a regular meeting the following month, commanding officers of both MAG-13 and MAG-31, both Generals, plus our own CO, Colonel Reisweber, included this problem in the meeting's agenda. The Generals decided that flight pay could not be given to me since it would require they make an official request for such to Navy Hqtrs in DC. This could be of great embarrassment to the Generals, since regulation had it that, before shipping overseas, every Marine Air Group should have on its roster a qualified bombsight and autopilot mechanic. Hey, what happened to Lt. Bunny Paulis? Could be that he was a phony, possibly a friend of one of the Generals. Rather than face this dilemma, they opted for a much easier way out: that was to compensate me in two entirely different ways. First, I would be promoted to Staff Sargent. That wasn't hard to take since recently, on September 13, I had been promoted to the rank of Sargent. Second, I could, at any time and at no cost to me, be given easy access to liquor. This was real easy for them to implement. The liquor would come from the officers larder.

The officers had all they wanted, and an occasional bottle would never be missed. To have good booze for free just by asking might look like a panacea for me, in contrast to all other enlisted men having to fend for themselves. Like an obedient young Marine, I went along with their decision. No flight pay? OK. Extra pay wouldn't ever be missed, since there existed no place out here for me to spend it. On the other hand, wearing those S/Sgt. stripes should make me feel pretty good. Under ordinary circumstances I would have had to wait many more months for that promotion. And how about the booze? Well, I would have much preferred a simple, steady supply of ordinary cold beer. I was now about one week away from my 19th birthday, and still had not found hard liquor very appealing.

Here on Samoa, this situation could likely make me very popular among the enlisted men. I now had good American booze at my disposal, anytime I wanted. Lt. Camper mentioned that I should be careful in how I handled this new bonanza, but knew me well enough to have complete confidence in me. I would not abuse the privilege. I drank the free stuff only occasionally, and since I was now bunking an isolated life in the jungle with two mature Marines, I quietly shared the booze only with them. This setup of delivering each a bottle of booze seemed to me a little weird; I had only to casually mention a bottle when in the presence of Lt. Camper, and that evening I would be sure to find a bottle neatly tucked under the pillow on my bunk. In the end, I never did acquire a taste for liquor, at least not while I was overseas. Subsequently, on January 01, 1944, I received the prestigious promotion to Staff Sargent, thus now making me a senior NCO… A great way to start the New Year!

Ask any Marine what he thought of the chow served at Marine bases in the States and overseas. Lousy, would be his typical answer. On the other hand, personnel at all Navy bases were customarily treated to the best of chow. When this young Marine was occasionally stationed at a Navy base, he found the chow to be excellent, without exception. It was heard that some Marines volunteered duty at forlorn Navy establishments or undesirable ships, just in order to take advantage of the fine chow served there.

During the war, feeding all the troops spread throughout the many bases in the vast Pacific was indeed a formidable task. I had the privilege of visiting many small islands in the South-Central Pacific.

Everywhere I found a shortage of good chow, even at those bases well behind the front lines. On several of these trips, we visitors simply had to go hungry, or at best, be served very small portions of the good stuff. There just wasn't enough to go around. On one particular occasion at our airbase on American Samoa, the mess officer somehow came into possession of a small supply of genuine steaks. But there was a problem. There weren't enough steaks to make a complete meal for the Marines stationed at this compound, even if portions were shaved down a bit. But, this crafty officer was able to come up with a solution to this problem. He would save this treat for one particular day of the year, and that was Good Friday of the 1943 Easter season. He sensibly reasoned that no Marine of Catholic faith would touch this meat treat. And he was right! I had a strict Catholic upbringing and along with many others, simply passed up this tempting offering. The remaining troops then had their modest fill, thus leaving the mess officer feeling he had successfully solved the problem. That is, until the base Chaplain got wind of it and was furious! He wanted the mess officer court martialed. But, cooler heads did prevail, and without further issue, the Marines dutifully returned to tending to their daily tasks.

However, a more permanent solution was soon to present itself. From the great continent of Australia, we started receiving regular shipments of lamb. And it wasn't long before we were eating lamb for supper every day. Only, this meat was not truly lamb, as that from young sheep. Our lamb was really mutton, derived from old and bigger sheep,... most likely rams. And it always carried with it a faint, but distinct, unpleasant odor. Nevertheless, the servings of mutton persisted day after day, with no end in sight. Eventually, we responded by simply refusing to take the mutton on our trays as we passed along the chow line. This then was compounded with the addition of mutton to our daily lunch menu. Where would this end? There seemed no solution. Something had to be done! Obviously, our base being 1,900 miles from the front lines left us in a poor bargaining position for any good food in the area. Finally, we troops saw a way of putting a stop to this endless supply of unwanted meat. We all proceeded to take mutton onto our trays as we passed through the chow line, and then to simply dump it into the trash can. This plan at first seemed to work, but after a while, evidence showed that the huge supply of mutton stored in the kitchen's coolers was starting to smell, evidence of going bad. This situation now demanded getting rid of it altogether. The brass then decided the only way to do this was to haul it out to sea on barges and dump it overboard.

But this wasn't the end of the story. Apparently, the Navy barges did not travel far enough offshore before dumping their unpleasant load. That same night when the tide changed to an incoming one, big legs of mutton started washing ashore, and there were lots of them! The officials were left dumbfounded and spent the entire day trying to decide what to do. In the meanwhile, tons of mutton lay exposed to the searing tropical sun. By evening, the stench became so bad that all troops had to evacuate along the shoreline and move inland. The brass finally made their move and rounded up a work detail of trustworthy natives, armed them with ten foot long spiked poles, and had them canvass the entire coastline, skewering every carcass, and then load them onto trucks for delivery to the docks at Pago Pago. There, waiting barges hauled this highly unwanted cargo a full ten miles out to sea before dumping it a final time. And this time the mutton thankfully stayed out at sea.

Finally, this smelly mutton war was over. The Marines had triumphed once again, albeit having to go a bit hungry for a while. Very likely, a similar scenario must have played itself out in other areas of the war in the Pacific. Having to eat K rations and Spam really wasn't that bad after all. The memory of this malodorous mutton incident had such a profound and lasting effect on this young Marine that, for many years after the war, he was unable to get himself into tasting or eating of the tenderest of any prepared lamb.

The ocean was also used as a dumping ground for one other particular item, and that was old ammunition. Occasionally, my department would receive a directive from headquarters in Washington, DC to dispose of, or technically, to survey specific lot numbers of outdated ordnance, primarily 50 caliber ammo, belt loaded for use in our fighter and bomber planes. Instructions were to barge them out to sea (no specific distance) and simply dump them overboard. Instructions never elaborated on the need for this drastic action, except at times to mention that it was outdated. In retrospect, I believe that this stuff was so old that it may have become too dangerous to use. I remember from personal experience that at the outbreak of WW II, the Navy and Marine Corps were somewhat saddled with obsolete warplanes and small arms. Hence it followed that once our war industry back home got in high gear and started producing vast supplies at a phenomenal rate, the old stuff we were storing here in Samoa simply had to go. I recall one directive instructing me to get rid of approximately one million rounds of belt loaded ammo.

Walt Augustyniak, Fiji Islands, South Pacific, 1944

In the middle of one of these work details of loading the ammo to be trucked to the harbor, our work crew decided to turn this boring chore into a little R&R. We set up a 50 caliber machine gun at the end of one of the airport runways, and then pulled a couple of condemned boxes of ammo from the truck. This ammo was belt loaded such that it held interspersed rounds of tracer shells. The plan was to fire a burst of rounds at a passing wave, look for the fiery trail left by a tracer shell, and then try to intercept that fast moving target with the use of the fiery trail left by the tracer shells being dispensed in a following burst of fire. It was fun for a while, but the novelty soon began to wear off.

However, a new challenge did on occasion present itself... that of a stray sea gull venturing into our line of fire, instantly becoming fair game. Now, before any of today's bird and animal lovers become incensed over this long past practice, I must sheepishly admit that we never did score a direct hit, or shoot down one of these poor, defenseless "enemy aircraft." It was just another way for lonely troops to inject a little fun in their daily routine.

17. TAKING TARAWA, THE GILBERTS & THE MARSHALLS

In late 1942, with the campaign in the Solomons starting to turn in our favor, plans for moving into the Japanese held Marshall and Gilbert Islands in the North Pacific were initiated. At the time, our Navy was not quite ready to take on Japan's still formidable fleet of warships. We started with a hit and run tactic on an island in the Gilbert Island chain. On August 17, 1942, in heavy seas, two Marine Companies from the 2nd Raider Battalion were dropped off by submarine into motor-powered rubber boats and made a landing on lightly defended Makin, just north of the stronghold island of Tarawa. They were met with strong resistance from the Japanese defenders and suffered many casualties. Later that day, the Japanese brought in reinforcements by air. Fierce fighting caused the Marines to abandon their positions and attempt return to the sub. In the end, 18 Marines were killed, and 12 more found themselves unable to fight their way back to the rendezvous. Nine of them were left behind, captured, then transferred to another Japanese held island and later executed. After the war ended, the site was revisited and 19 graves were located and unearthed. These graves showed the Marines, fully clothed and still holding their rifles. The friendly natives had reverently buried them in a remote area on the island. This raid produced another negative effect. In addition to failing to divert some Japanese forces out of the Solomons, it unfortunately resulted in the Japanese proceeding to further fortify their positions on their main island of Tarawa.

Two months later, in hopes of lessening a Japanese defense buildup in this area, and promote a later, successful invasion against key islands in the Gilbert chain, US forces again tried a similar diversionary operation, this time on New Britain, an island bordering the Solomons. The Japanese took the bait and proceeded to bolster their naval forces in the Solomons at the expense of their positions in the Gilberts. In May of 1943, in preparation for a planned near-future offensive into the Gilbert Island chain, combined Marine and Army forces invaded and took back the Aleutian island of Attu. It was a sloppy operation, resulting in much higher casualties than expected. Consequently, invasion of the more fortified island of Kiska was put off until a greater U.S. force could be amassed. This invasion finally did take place on August 15, but to everyone's embarrassment found the island empty; it having been completely evacuated under the cover of fog at night.

Then in early November of 1943, the island of Abemama, just south of Tarawa, recently received special attention in the planning of the general assault on the Gilbert Island group. At that time, the US Navy submarine Nautilus took aboard a contingent of 68 Marines from a specially trained Amphibious Recon Group to deliver them to the beaches of Abemama. This would prove to be the first such recon action carried out by Marines in WW II. Their mission was to determine the size of the island's defense force and to subsequently mark beaches and channels for its ensuing invasion and that of the grand invasion of neighboring Tarawa. The mission almost ended in disaster when on November 19, their surfaced sub was sighted by the USS cruiser, the Santa Fe, which mistakenly had taken it for an enemy vessel and proceeded to fire on the helpless sub. One five inch shell did hit the sub's conning tower. Even though the shell proved to be a dud, it did damage by causing some flood waters to enter the tower. The sub took to safety by diving to 300 feet, where the damage was repaired, and then amazingly was able to proceed on its appointed mission.

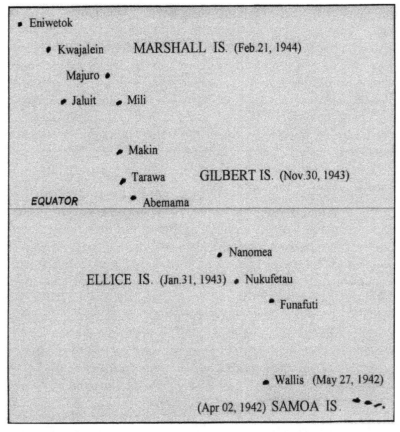

- Eniwetok
- Kwajalein   MARSHALL IS. (Feb.21, 1944)
  Majuro •
- Jaluit   • Mili

- Makin
- Tarawa   GILBERT IS. (Nov.30, 1943)
EQUATOR   • Abemama

- Nanomea
ELLICE IS. (Jan.31, 1943) • Nukufetau
                              • Funafuti

- Wallis (May 27, 1942)
(Apr 02, 1942) SAMOA IS.

A MAP SHOWING DATES OF UNCONTESTED U.S. FORCES
OCCUPYING NEUTRAL ISLANDS IN THE SOUTH CENTRAL
PACIFIC, AND OF BATTLE-CAPTURED ENEMY ISLANDS IN
THE NORTH CENTRAL PACIFIC

A day or two later, the raiding party found itself outside the
island's reef and was able to put a landing party ashore without
drawing fire from enemy forces. They were delighted to meet just a
group of friendly natives, who informed the recon party that the
defending Japanese garrison consisted of only 25 heavily armed men,
who were now entrenched on a neighboring spit of an island. The
raiding party advanced and made light contact with the entrenched
enemy, but then decided to call it a day and retire to a safer position.

The next day the party returned, but encountered very heavy
enemy fire which resulted in the death of one Marine and the serious

wounding of another. Again the party decided to withdraw its assault force. When they returned the following morning, they were met by another native with the astounding news that all the Japanese soldiers were now dead. He told the wild story of the Japanese commander, who, while conducting a rant and rave pep talk urged his troops to kill all the "American devils," took to wildly swinging his pistol about. Somehow, the pistol accidentally went off and mortally wounded him. The leaderless troops now found themselves in a hopeless situation, and unanimously decided to commit mass suicide. The recon party went ashore and verified this, then withdrew, leaving the island essentially now in American hands.

The next day, November 17, 1943, an unchallenged US Naval fleet assembled off the beaches of Betio, the main island of the Tarawa chain on which a finished runway had already existed. The fleet delivered a relentless bombardment of the islands defenses, being accompanied by air sorties carried out by carrier-based fighter planes and dive bombers. At 9 AM, the first wave of Marines hit the beaches of Betio, suffering only a few casualties. The second wave, coming in to land on Red Beach, and using Higgins boats, did not fare so well. These boats required four to five feet of water in order to successfully navigate. Because the available tide information for these islands was grossly incorrect, none of these boats made it to the landing beaches, with most becoming hung up on submerged coral reefs. Their Marine occupants were forced to abandon, disembark into waist high waters and painstakingly make their way to the beaches, many hundred yards away. They proved easy targets for the enemy shore batteries. Here, Marine casualties ran very high. By nightfall, little progress had been made, with one stark message coming from the beaches that concluded: "Issue in doubt." It wasn't until noon on November 23 that enemy resistance on Tarawa and Makin was declared over. It was indeed a hard fought and costly battle.

At our air base in Samoa, the first bad news had trickled in with the arrival of two B-24s from the battle zone, carrying twenty combat injured troops for treatment at our 300 bed mobile hospital. The Navy had previously assured the Marine command that the intense bombardment from their ships would knock out all the enemy's defense positions. The military brass had been so sure of an easy victory, that previous arrangements made were to treat an estimated 200 casualties at our Samoan mobile hospital. Unfortunately, grim news followed telling of casualties running far beyond that figure. Further flights into Samoa carrying wounded Marines were summarily canceled, and casualties instead were collected by off-shore ships possessing basic medical dispensaries. These treated casualties were then transferred to a few fast moving ships and transported to major hospitals at Pearl Harbor. Surprisingly, no hospital ship had been included in the invading naval fleet. The intense fighting on the airfield side of the island lasted about 76 hours before the entire island was declared secure. One thousand Marines were reported to have lost their lives over this small, insignificant island. On Samoa, scuttlebutt had these figures grossly underestimated.

Meanwhile, on Samoa, ammo shipments from my depots in the jungle were being carried out at an almost feverish pace. I had to work my volunteer crews around the clock. I soon ran out of volunteers. When my main crew finally became exhausted, I was forced to enter our church services in search of fresh workers. And after that, in a last-ditch move of desperation, I invaded the mess hall and pulled cooks and kitchen hands from their work stations. They did not relish this new work assignment, expressing their discontent in no uncertain terms. When this all-out effort finally subsided about 48 hours later, all these workers were promptly released. During this time, I had not had a chance to catch any sleep. Suddenly finding myself all alone in my small office, I slumped down on my bunk and was out in no time. It wasn't very long before I found myself being shaken awake by a hunched over, very anxious Marine fighter pilot. I managed to sit up and ask what he wanted. As he answered, I just flopped back down and drifted back into a deep sleep. He tried to wake me once more. Somehow, I managed to wake up to the degree of learning that he was in dire need of a supply of starter cartridges for his plane. All small war planes operate without a battery that normally would be used to power-start the engine. Instead, a shotgun type shell is inserted into a special receptacle in the engine housing and literally fired. The force of the explosion is channeled to rotate the engine through several revolutions, and hopefully enough for it to catch, after which the engine generates its own power for the plane's operation. This time, I managed to stand up, mumble a few words of acknowledgement, then lose it, and once again plop back down on the bunk, dead to the world. With that, the frustrated Lt. finally gave up and marched off, presumably in search of finding someone else to fix him up with starter cartridges.

After the battle, ammo shipments to the battlefield area of the newly acquired Gilbert Island chain continued, but at a considerably slower pace. The danger of enemy aerial raids on Samoa had now literally disappeared. We no longer had to live under camouflage conditions. I immediately took advantage of this development by moving out of my temporary quarters deep in the jungle to return to living quarters adjacent to the airfield. I found an office recently vacated by a high ranking officer. The building was twice the size of our existing eight man fales, and as with all other buildings in the area, it was somewhat hidden by the naturally growing jungle vegetation. I found it fortunate to already have a bulldozer at my disposal. This vehicle was considered a necessity for moving shipments of ammo through the jungle trails during the rainy season. The road leading to all the twelve ammunition magazines was a winding, coarse trail which often became a sea of mud during the rainy season. The dozer's function was to pull trailers, laden with heavy loads of bombs and ammo through the poorly maintained jungle trail, then transfer the ammo to trucks bound for the docks in Pago Pago. This dozer came without a typical front blade, since that attachment was not needed for this type of work. However, I did manage to develop a way of tearing up the dense vegetation by pivoting the dozer on either of its tracks, swinging it back and forth. The wide metal tracks easily chewed up the vegetation. Then I used the tracks laterally to push the piles of vegetation to the sides. Boy, was this kid having fun!

I borrowed some tools and was able to preserve half of this building as my own little office and turned the rest into spacious and private living quarters. I built my bunk into the wall with the screening at bunk level, much the same as our existing fales. My own private hut! Now that's what I called luxury! I regaled in my new, little utopia, but my luxury was only to last for a week or so. Superior officers stepped in once more to deal me another blow. Recently a new air wing, the 4th Marine Base Defense Air Wing, had been formed, into which both MAG-13 and MAG-31 were folded. Now, a new commanding general was coming to Samoa from headquarters in

Ewa, Hawaii, to set up temporary headquarters and be closer to the front lines. My refurbished refuge had caught his eye. With my bulldozer, I had completely cleared about 50 feet of surrounding jungle vegetation. Along with my refurbished office section, this building very much looked suitable for his needs.

Without fanfare I was told to move out. No "sorry, pal" or "too bad, sonny." Because of the arrival of more MAG-31 personnel, I ended up having to move into an already full hut of 16 other Marines. But there was a small bright side to this fiasco, since my new bunkmates were ones I had come to know rather well over the past many months. So once more, I would get to enjoy some camaraderie. It was still much better than being stuck deep in the jungle away from my peers.

Meanwhile, little time was wasted in developing strong bases on our newly won islands of Tarawa, Abemama and Makin. In a short time, much of the neighboring Marshall Islands were earmarked for intense bombing raids. Some of these islands were large and heavily fortified. However, some smaller ones situated very close to the Gilberts, typically were not. On January 31, 1944, the same company of Amphibious Recon that had recently raided Abemama, now conducted a similar landing and raid on the small Marshall island of Majuro, and the island was secured that same day. Casualties ran only a fraction of those suffered at Tarawa. Kwajelein, which already had a functioning airstrip, was also invaded and both islands were secured by February 07. On February 19, the busy CBs quickly constructed a runway on Majuro, and finally on February 19, 1944, the esteemed MAG-13, which had been based on Tutuila since April, 1942, left Samoa for good for its new base of operations on Majuro. I bade a sad farewell to my good buddy, Leon Augustyn. He was finally getting off this island, but inauspiciously headed toward the front lines. Oh well, it was a step toward eventually getting on the road leading to home. Also, two other close-by Marshall Islands, Mille and Jaluit, were taken soon after and had runways quickly built on them by our ever busy CBs.

From Tarawa and these newly won Marshall Islands, larger enemy held island strongholds to the west were then relentlessly bombed and rendered useless as enemy strongholds. Eniwetok, the furthest west, fell to American forces on February 23. Planes and personnel from MAG-31 would eventually wind up stationed on the much larger atoll of Kwajalein. The next phase of the war effort would now move more successfully along a more direct path toward the Japanese mainland, except that enemy islands to be encountered would undoubtedly be of much larger size and most certainly more fiercely defended.

18. FLIGHT TO TARAWA WITH GENERAL PRICE

Back on Samoa on February 03, 1944, while I was having lunch at our mess hall, an excited PBY crew member barged in looking for me. He proceeded to grab me by the shoulder, blurting: "Let's go, Kelly. Our plane's autopilot needs working on and the General wants it fixed immediately." He was referring to Major General Charles F. B. Price, commander of the Marine defense forces in the immediate area. I said I needed some time to stop at my fale and grab some stuff. He replied that the plane was ready for a long flight, and waiting for me. "No time to grab some clothes and a tooth brush, or tell my superior, Lt. Camper, that I'm going somewhere?" "No, c'mon. There's no time for that." "How long are we going to be gone?" "I don't know. C'mon, the General's waiting." Oh, well, maybe I can have the problem fixed in a jiffy and get dropped off on an island along the way. "OK...let's go." Unbeknownst to me, the General was on his way for an extended inspection tour of our newly won islands in the Gilberts. I would not be made aware of this plan even as we headed directly for the waiting PBY. This tour would eventually take me away from my duties on Samoa for seven days!

The first leg of the journey of 3.3 hours took us to the nearby French island of Wallis. I had jumped on the autopilot problem as soon as we were airborne. It was a mechanical one in the stabilizer gyro, and a common occurrence. I had it fixed in less than an hour. I had now only to sit back and enjoy the ride. This should really be a treat. The only flights I had previously made were either over Tutuila or to Upolu, both of which took less than an hour. One negative aspect was that I had to stay confined to the bombardier's station in the nose of the plane, even on takeoff and landing. The General was a very dignified officer, always accompanied by his aides, a major and a captain, plus an impressive array of luggage. With our flight crew of two pilots, a radio operator/navigator, and a flight engineer/crew chief, there just wasn't any place left for me to plunk down in the main cabin. I would be in the way. So, in the nose I stayed. It was comfortable, even though I had no seat and felt cramped after a time. The nose of the plane had a shuttered window, expressly for use by the bombardier. So, I did enjoy a great view as we flew along, except that the view turned out to be a never ending featureless panorama of open seas.

I found the stopover at Wallis to be fascinating. Its landscape was rather unusual. It was larger than the average atoll, with an unusually large land mass of several square miles in the center, whereas a coral atoll was typically comprised of a sprawling central lagoon surrounded by a wispy chain or ring of coral outcroppings, with only a few of them big enough to support any small population. Regarding one of Wallis' small islands, a story circulated that was a little hard to believe. It told of a leper colony located there, run by French missionaries. A narrow causeway from the main island made it accessible. Servicemen were cautioned to never go there. If you did, you might then have to spend the next seven years in quarantine in order to assure that you had not contracted the Leprosy disease.

We found it fascinating to watch incoming or departing planes come down the long runway and then all of a sudden simply drop out of sight! A brief moment of concern would pass before the plane would magically reappear, as if jumping directly out of the ground. The airport had a deep dip in the middle of the runway section. Evidently, making it flat would have required unavailable landfill, plus time and effort in the construction process. As such, the really big and heavy four engine bombers never got to use it. Among servicemen, this island just wasn't a popular place. One squadron historian was later to note "Wallis has gained the reputation as the best spot on God's earth to keep away from." Whereas nearby Upolu Island offered servicemen the exactly opposite reputation. Another incidental memory stuck in my mind over the years. That was of a small native waif who hung around the airbase. He was about eight years old, and likely an orphan. He would greet every incoming flight crew with a big smile, a cigar hanging out of his mouth and a "Howya doin', Joe?" He addressed everyone as Joe, chattered endlessly, and was always in search of a handout.

We left Wallis the same day and for some reason flew back to the Samoas, only this time to Upolu. I couldn't understand this route change. Upolu had to be one of his inspection stops, but could have been pulled off in a more successive order. Previously, after I had fixed the autopilot, I had sheepishly inquired as to whether the plane could fly back to Tutuila and drop me off. This would be a less than one hour flight. However, the General's agenda precluded all others. I stayed put. He had decided that I ultimately must stay aboard for the entire trip, in case more autopilot problems were to crop up. Also, if I were to be left off at Upolu, the chances of grabbing a plane ride back to Tutuila might be slim, since planes flying in this route were routinely single-seaters. Now with daylight fading fast, the crew was delighted to learn we were staying here for the night.

The landing at Upolu had revealed a ritual that would take place several more times whenever we visited a new island: the General's luggage. The General would first disembark from the plane along with his two aides. Then the flight crew would toss out the General's complete repertoire of baggage, some six to eight valises and handbags. The PBY's main body was the shape of a big pontoon, since that's what it really was. The baggage compartment was in the bottom of the pontoon and most easily accessed through a hatch on its upper surface. So the stream of valises would come popping out of this hatch and then come rattling down the side of the pontoon. The two aides would catch them, very neatly line them up, and the General would then ceremoniously walk past them, pointing at this one, that one, etc. These bags would then be loaded into a waiting command car, and all would speed off for some cozy overnight accommodations. The rest of the bags were then tossed back aboard the plane. Meanwhile, we three lonely crewmen stayed with the plane and its cramped quarters, protecting it from who knows what.

The next day we headed north again, stopping at Wallis once more. Again, our little native waif friend was there to greet us. The PBY's flight range was typically five hours. These past local flights were 2.5 to 3.5 hours in duration. Maybe the General needed to often stretch his legs, but more likely he had simply forgotten something. In flying directly over a sparsely populated stretch of ocean, it was rather easy to miss your target. So, breaking the flight into shorter segments greatly enhanced the chances of hitting your intended airfield. This sort of misfortune was experienced recently by the same pilot of this flight, veteran Captain Whitey Hobbs. Hobbs was what you would call an old salt. Sporting a completely white head of hair, Whitey went way back in Marine Corps aviation history. Word had it that he had graduated from Navy flight school as a PFC! This story could have a real basis, since there are vague references found in some early aviation records that some pilots graduating flight school at that time may have been given this mediocre rank.

The getting-lost story went on to describe a previous five-plus hour flight to an area a little further north of our present position. As the plane neared its destination area, the sought island was nowhere to be seen. Whitey then briefly took over the navigator's seat, a move he often did. It was often said that Whitey had little trust in his crew, since he was known for often taking over each one of their tasks. He had tremendous knowledge about everything that had to do with flying. Oddly, I was somehow immune to his overbearing trait. He would occasionally use the bombsight as a tool for getting a good bearing for navigation calculations, but never toyed with autopilot problems. After a brief reassessment of his navigation figures, he determined they were lost and to continue flying the same course might take them even further off target. With daylight rapidly fading, the chances of finding their target destination was becoming more remote. Whitey decided it would be better to put the plane down in the sea for the night, right then and there, and to wait for daylight. He did just that, with the crew having to bail water all through the night. During open ocean landings, amphibious planes often sprung leaks, accumulating water in their bilge section. The next morning, all hands eagerly awaited Whitey's next move. After a quick review of his navigation figures, he pointed a finger at a specific spot on the horizon and then promptly took off on that heading. Much to everyone's delight, it wasn't long before their tiny island target crept into full view.

After spending very little time on Wallis, we promptly embarked on a 3.5 hour flight for the main island in the Ellice Island chain, Funafuti. This was my first experience visiting a conventional coral atoll island. The perimeter of the coral formation was large, but the land mass it contained was rather small. In spite of its small size, Funafuti showed lots of activity. At the airfield, the island was only a half mile wide. It seemed to me you could throw a stone across it. There were planes all over the place. The US Air Corps had two B-24 air groups stationed there and kept busy with daily, long range bombing raids on Tarawa. Also, Marines kept fighter planes and dive bombers stationed there, but strictly for defense purposes. However, these were not kept very busy since Japanese bomber raids were infrequent, only about once a month. The monotony was well expressed in one operational report from this area which simply stated: "Enemy activity in the Central Pacific was conspicuous by its absence."

We were to spend the night on Funafuti and the crew was once again treated to watching the ritual of the handling of the General's baggage. All the officers again spent the night away from the plane, whereas the crew had to fend for themselves for chow, and then yet again bunk down inside the PBY. While the crew had time to pack a bag, I was on day three without a toothbrush or a change of clothes. The next day we headed northward to inspect the next island in the Ellice chain, Nanomea, the northernmost island and closest to Tarawa and the Gilberts. At about 300 miles from the main base at Funafuti, this coral island was rather condensed in its spread, and had practically no central lagoon as compared to Funafuti with its huge sprawling lagoon. Being closest to Tarawa made it a busy place. In addition to Navy fighter and dive bomber squadrons, two medium range US Air Corps bomber squadrons were also there for conducting air raids on Tarawa. Several squadrons of Marine Corps fighters also helped defend the island during infrequent enemy air raids.

We spent the night there before leaving the next morning for Tarawa, our final destination. Our arrival at Tarawa turned out to be quite a memorable one. As our PBY approached the airbase, a flight of five F4F Marine fighter planes swooped out of the sky and proceeded to escort our PBY over the airbase. What a greeting! I was delighted. Even though Tarawa was declared secure some ten weeks prior, raids from the nearby Japanese-held Marshall Islands remained a possibility. We were still in the war zone. Our landing on the pock-marked runway exposed a sobering sight. The overall terrain revealed the strain of recent, heavily pitched battles. Almost every palm and coconut tree was stripped of its foliage. The dead had long since been taken away or buried in soft, sandy mass graves.

The General took his time inspecting the facilities, so the crew and I were able to roam around the small island looking over the beaches where most of the carnage had taken place. I broke off after a short while and did a solitary, slow and solemn tour of the battle areas. Bunkers that housed the stubborn Japanese defenders were now all just mounds of sand. On one end of the island stood a poised eight inch cannon put out of action by our heavy naval bombardment. My attention was focused on finding the famed Red Beach, which had sustained the heaviest casualties. The beach itself was still littered with debris of every sort. Conspicuously absent were souvenir items, such as Japanese flags, guns, sabers, etc. There was, however, one Japanese souvenir that was quite abundant and that was the many empty sake wine bottles. I first assumed they had been consumed by the Japanese, possibly prior to embarking one of their infamous suicide charges. However, this idea later was termed foolish by veteran Marine, Tim Shawaryn, from South Jersey whom I had met in 2013, and who had participated and survived that landing and the following 62 hour battle. He assured me that it was Marines who had emptied those wine bottles. To the victor belonged the spoils. I did manage to find and keep one Japanese combat accessory as a lasting souvenir, and that was a hand grenade pouch, made out of recycled rubber tire tread and worn on one's belt. In the shallow lagoon facing the beach, there floated countless disabled amphibious vehicles, mostly Higgins boats, which had become hung up on the shallow water coral outcroppings. To me, the abandoned watercraft appeared so numerous that I imagined it possible to literally hop from one to the next across the entire lagoon.

The island was rather crowded with personnel. Securing food could be a real problem for visitors. The officers always fared well, but we enlisted crew men were left to fend for ourselves. Up until now, we hadn't had anything that resembled a meal for the last three days. The hunger pangs had already faded and were now replaced by an ever present empty-gut gnawing feeling and accompanied by a dull, lingering headache. Along the way, we did manage to mooch some K rations from local troops. But, on this day we finally did get to sit at a table and enjoy a regular mess hall meal. It consisted of a small portion (maybe two ounces) of meat, and two dabs of vegetables. Later in the day, the General decided that spending the night on Tarawa might not be wise, since the island was still under potential air raids from remaining enemy held islands. For safety's sake, we hopped back on the plane and took off for a 100 mile flight to the neighboring captured island of Abemama. We learned that during the original occupation of the island on November 20, the Navy CBs had landed along with the Marines and immediately proceeded to carve an airstrip out of the island's jungle. Forty eight hours later, our fighter planes were able to use the new runway. A few weeks later, heavy steel matting was installed on its surface. Our PBY had the privilege of being the first large airplane to land on this island's new runway.

With little or no amenities, we did however spend a safe night there. This island was situated exactly on the equator, with conditions of very high heat and humidity. For the previous three nights we had slept on mattresses inside the plane, but not on this night. We dragged our mattresses out of the side blister, up and onto the top of the PBY's flat and very broad wing. This move went well until about three AM, when the typical late night tropical rains came pouring down. A fast retreat was made back inside, where we wisely decided to rough it out. The next day we were visited by local natives, and noticed that the women all had bath towels strung across their bare chests, with the ends deftly tucked in under their armpits. On every newly won island, the Navy casually handed out tee shirts for the native women to wear, thus keeping their bare chests covered. At Abemama, we were left to assume the Navy had temporarily run out of tee shirts.

The next day we took off for a short visit back to Nanomea. The reasons for these frequent backtracking trips were never revealed to us enlisted men. Officers very seldom let us in on what was going on. Also, this trip was meant for inspection, and the General must have had his reasons. These small islands really had nothing to offer as far as luxuries and such. So, the stay was short and we departed that afternoon for the last island in the Ellice group, Nukufetau. This island too was smaller than Funafuti. Its outlying atoll, unlike all the other atolls visited, had a very unusual shape, that of an almost a perfect rectangle. This island's air base also held a squadron of US Air Corps bombers as well as Marine fighter planes. Another feature of this island that also got my attention was that of the pronounced odor of dead fish. Having to spend an overnight there made this stink much more pronounced and easier to remember.

The next day, General Price decided he needed to revisit Funafuti, which went without incident. Finally, our tour was over and we once again headed south, but this time across the open seas directly back to Samoa. It would take in excess of five flying hours and we had the capability of doing it. However, for safety's sake, the General had us stop at Wallis, where we again spent a night, and then to Upolu where we spent another night. Finally, on February 10, 1944, after spending seven days and nights on this journey, we touched down at our home base on Tutuila. We enlisted men now looked forward to downing a solid meal, taking a real shower, and hitting our bunks for some well-deserved sleep. Lt. Camper, my ordnance officer was very glad to have me back. He had not been made aware of my sudden departure until the day after I was gone. Fortunately, during my absence, activity at the ammunition depot had not been very demanding, thus allowing me to quickly catch up on the work load.

19. TRIP TO FIJI

With all operating squadrons now having shifted north to the new front lines, the members of MCAF suddenly found themselves all alone on Tutuila. On the bright side, the new Air Commander who had recently had me evicted from my jazzy quarters had also departed and set up his headquarters much closer to the fast moving war zone. I wasted no time moving back into my cozy former home/office. Idle time suddenly became more available, although our two PBYs were being kept quite busy, which in turn, kept me a bit busy. And so, on February 20, 1944, I again found myself being whisked away from my regular ammunition depot duties and taken aboard a five hour flight, this time bound for the Fiji Islands, some 800 miles to the west and directly on the southern sea/air route to Australia. Only this time, there was ample time to gather my personal gear and also to inform Lt. Camper that I would be gone for a few days.

I was delighted to find that salty Captain Hobbs would once again be our pilot. This time there were no dignitaries aboard, just the two pilots, a two man crew, and myself, the expert autopilot specialist so sought after on these long flights over empty Pacific Ocean waters. Without a dignitary aboard, we made the five hour flight without a stopover. I had the autopilot fixed in the first hour of flight and was able to bask in this new relaxed atmosphere. Of much more significance, however, was that I discovered Fiji was a large volcanic island, but unlike Samoa, was highly developed. In the 15 months I had already spent in the South Pacific, I was the only enlisted man from MCAF to have had the good fortune of getting off Samoa and seeing some of the other (good and bad) neighboring islands.

We landed rather late in the day at the airport at the village of Nausori, just outside the capital city of Suva, on the main island of Viti Levu. In view of the late hour, and since we were scheduled to spend three overnights here, Captain Hobbs suggested the crew stay with the plane the first night. There would be plenty of time left for us to live it up in Suva. Of course, he and his copilot wasted no time in high-tailing it into town. Before he left, Captain Hobbs cautioned us to not overdo it when doing liberty in Suva. Otherwise, he might be tempted to suggest a hangover cure, which would be for us clean the plane's bilge. As with any typical watercraft, the PBY accumulated water leakages brought about during occasional sea landings. The obnoxious odor of long trapped bilge water would not fare well with a pounding hangover. For now, we were treated with good chow and appreciated spending the night at a nearby defense air base with crews from a contingent of Marine fighter planes that were stationed there.

The PBY crew – Walt MacMillan, and Rufus "Buck" Barton

The next morning found us aboard a taxi headed for Suva. It was quite a shock to suddenly find ourselves deep within a bustling, modern city. Multi story buildings stood all about, including hotels, department stores and night clubs. This sure looked like civilization, and should make for a memorable liberty. My two companions were the PBY's regular crew members: Walt MacMillan, the crew chief, and Rufus Barton, the radioman/navigator. We first took in some sightseeing and picking up souvenirs for home. One of the first scenes we came across was that of a native policeman, standing in the center of the city's crossroads, directing traffic. He was dressed in native gear, that is, a short skirt (or sulu) and a plain sleeveless shirt. But what was most striking was his hairdo. He sported a genuine Afro, teased out into a huge ball. Fiji is located in the region of the South Pacific referred to as Melanesia. Natives here were more dark-skinned than those in nearby Polynesia, and obviously descendants of a slightly different race. As we coursed through some of the shops and other establishments, we noticed that the proprietors were all Indian, from Southeast Asia. The story told to us was that when the British first took over this island country, they found the natives were too wild to learn domestic and manual skills. So the British simply brought in legions of workers from India to fulfill these tasks. The natives did eventually learn these skills, and were able to perform all the domestic and manual jobs, thus freeing the Indian workers to become the island's shop and business owners.

The next stop on our list was to visit a photo shop to have pictures taken for sending home. A personal telegram could also be sent home, but because of strict censorship, we were restricted to selecting a short message from an approved list. It would go something like: "Hi Mom, I'm doing OK. I miss you very much and hope to be home soon." Sounds good, doesn't it? Well, I selected one of these and in no time at all, my telegram was sent off to my parents. Upon my return to the States many months later, I was to learn that the telegram was delivered to them in the middle of the night. My parents were from the old country and did not understand the significance of such a late hour communication. They feared the worst. In the recent past, they heard of neighbors receiving a telegram from the government with news of their son having been killed in action. The Fiji islands happen to lie on the other side of the International Dateline, somehow causing the telegram's delivery to take place in the USA at this late hour. The news scared my parents half to death, and it wasn't until later in the day that a neighbor would clarify the situation. A few days later, when viewing the photo I had sent by mail from Fiji, their concern was once again tested after noting the stark look that I presented.

As evening started to settle in, it was time to start making the rounds at the many bars in town. Somewhere along the line we picked up another young Marine for company. The bars were all in high-end hotels. Wine was the drink most served. Liquor seemed scarce, and since I had not as yet become an accomplished drinker, I once again found myself thrust into the role of a watchdog, while my drinking pals had a ball. Walt MacMillan was a bit more mature and reserved than the rest of us. This was typical of a crew chief, since he carried a lot of responsibility in keeping the plane airworthy. As the evening wore on, a disturbing pattern began to emerge as Rufus started to become somewhat belligerent. Obviously, the many drinks he had consumed were turning him into a very combative person. As he sat at the table, he would fix his sight at a person sitting across the room, then suddenly jump up, saying... "That guy over there is bothering me!" We tried everything to distract him. Eventually, he would calm down, but only for a while, and then once again, he'd flare up. At one point, he jumped up and started to charge across the room to confront this imaginary nemesis. Again, Walt and I had to physically restrain him, and get him to come back and sit down.

Finally, this local ruckus got the attention of the (female) maître d`, who must have been watching us. Only now she was looking directly at Rufus. Seeing this, Rufus jumped up again, and started to go directly at her. Once again we restrained him, only this time the maître d` insisted that we leave. That we did while trying to get Rufus calmed down. We sweet-talked him into being a good boy so we could continue having a good time somewhere else. He agreed and we then hit another bar. But the calm was not to last. Rufus became agitated once more, and to the point where we were just about to be physically ejected. We found ourselves outside once again. What to do now? We had to forget about more bars, but it was too early to call it an evening. We then hailed a cab hoping to find a part of town where bars might be a bit more tolerant toward raucous servicemen. The four of us climbed in and were greeted by a "Where to, guys?" With this, Rufus reared up, loudly proclaiming: "Take us to a cat house. I wanna get a piece of ass." The driver shook his head for a few seconds, and then calmly proceeded to speed off towards the outskirts of town. When I heard cat house and realized where we were headed, out into the bush in search of prostitutes, I near panicked. This did not look good - a bad situation - one definitely to be avoided. There seemed no way out. For the moment, I managed to dutifully stay silent.

We hadn't traveled very far when the cabbie spied a SP (shore patrol) canvassing the area. He immediately brought the cab to a screeching halt, jumped out, and excitedly blurted out to the SPs that these Marines were forcing him to take us to a whore house. Oh Boy! Saved by the bell! ...Or, were we? Here were two very intent shore patrolmen now rapidly approaching the cab with its four beleaguered Marines still inside. We immediately realized we had to get the hell out of there, and fast. Simultaneously, all doors flew open with four very concerned Marines spilling out and dashing in four different directions. The shore patrol didn't bother to pursue us, since they had accomplished their mission, and that was to save the cabbie and prevent us from getting into further trouble. Since we four renegades found ourselves still inside the city, we managed to find each other, and most important, to convince Rufus that the partying was over. In retrospect, I should mention that Rufus was a full blooded American Indian. The adage about Indians not being able to handle their liquor must hold some truth. Among the MAG-13 personnel on Samoa was the son of an Indian chief. His demeanor was also that of a chief, always conducting himself in an almost aristocratic manner. When later told of this incident, he reluctantly acknowledged that many of his people did possess this weakness. Here, in Suva, without further incident, we were able to finally call it a day, hustle back to our hotel room, and get a good night's sleep, ensuring that we'd be in good shape for the return to our plane the next day.

The next morning, with clear minds we stood ready to go. We first picked up our finished photos taken two days prior, and then got a cab for the return trip to the Nausori airport. Captain Hobbs joined us soon after. Following a quick assessment of the crew's mental faculties, he casually suggested the bilge be cleaned. With three of us attending, the task wouldn't be too unpleasant, but the two regular crew members spared me from having to crawl down into the stinky bilge. As we were about to leave the airfield, our young and inexperienced copilot begged permission to do the actual takeoff. Captain Hobbs always reserved this privilege for himself, but this time he reluctantly assented. With the copilot at the wheel, the plane sped down the open field, but soon started to wander to the right, racing off the prescribed flight path and crossing through and knocking down a few of a line of landing lights sticking out of the ground. We now found ourselves heading toward the perimeter bushes that marked the airport boundary. The Captain didn't waste any time in taking over, grabbing the wheel and managing to keep the plane on a path parallel to the runway. Fortunately, the smoothness of that area of the field ultimately allowed for a successful take-off.

The flight back was once again without any stopovers or incidents. But, as we approached the Tafuna runway, the Captain felt like he needed to announce our arrival. He decided that we should buzz the runway, that is, come in with throttles wide open, flying barely above the runway and then jauntily peeling off and up, just like fighter planes would customarily do after returning from a successful mission. You have to remember, fighter planes as well as dive bombers can ordinarily reach airspeeds of 300 miles per hour in such a maneuver. However, by design, the PBY is a bulky plane designed for cruising while carrying out air patrols. Its normal cruising speed is about 125 mph. Even if put it into a dive, you couldn't get much more out of the big bird. Instead of a steep dive, we had to settle for coming in at a moderate glide angle, but still with the throttles wide open as would be used in takeoffs, maybe reaching airspeed of 150 mph. The whole idea was to create a lot of noise and attract lots of attention on the ground. This it did, and we crew members thoroughly enjoyed the show. Then as we swung around for the routine touchdown, I noticed the Captain perform another of his rituals, which was to have a freshly lit cigarette propped in his mouth as he came in for the final approach. I suppose this was his way of relieving the tension associated with safely bringing down a big plane like the PBY. I had noticed this ritual on previous flights leading to Tarawa, but was not aware that the cigarette lighting-up ritual was a must do.

20. ABOARD A RESCUE MISSION

On Tutuila, as weeks rolled by and activities continued to wane, Lt. Camper took note of my recent extra responsibilities. I had been rather busy lately with the frequent repairing of PBY autopilot systems. He felt that something should be written in my records attesting to the additional duties I had been assuming. He asked our Colonel Reisweber if he would sign a citation attesting to my extra efforts. The Colonel said he would, and so Lt. Camper told me to write up what I felt was appropriate. The Colonel said he would sign it regardless of what was written. I did so, and the Colonel signed it without going over its contents. Similar to what he had been doing over the past 15 months regarding my monthly reports on ammunition transactions which were submitted to Naval Headquarters in DC.

On March 05, an emergency call came in to our airbase via the Navy radio station in Pago Pago, relating a distress call they had just received from a radio outpost on the small island of Manua, just 60 miles east of Tutuila. This radio post was manned 24 hours a day by two Navy personnel whose job it was to report any and all ship activities occurring within sight of that island. However, this report related that one of the island's senior native chiefs had become seriously ill as a result of a fall from a tree several days before. The radiomen stated that the chief needed hospital treatment to survive. He had several broken bones, and was now swollen and very feverish. Even though Manua was only 60 miles away by sea, it was determined that he could not survive the bumpy, open sea boat ride. So, it was decided to use a PBY to fly him back to our mobile hospital.

With my having a light work load at the time, I saw an opportunity to gain the experience of participating in a typical PBY air-sea rescue. Having to fix an autopilot would not be an issue this time, since this flight would take less than an hour. Many months prior, I was being considered for boarding a rescue flight bound for the Tonga Islands to the south. A strong earthquake had just created disaster conditions on one of its islands, and that government wished to evacuate dignitaries from the island. Unfortunately for me, I was scratched at the last minute. This time however, my plea was successfully received. Lt. Green would be our pilot. He was a young pilot with whom I had previously flown several times on local flights in the fall of 1943, each time to fix a malfunctioning autopilot. But he sure wasn't the seasoned pilot that Hobbs was. We also took aboard two medical professionals.

The flight to Manua took only 45 minutes. The main island of Tau painted a very pretty picture as viewed from the air, compact and lush with vegetation, just perched there, surrounded by crystal clear blue Pacific waters. It bore all the markings of an island paradise. It was a rectangular shaped island and not coral formed, but of volcanic origin, just like all the other larger islands in the Samoa group. It sported a central mountain peak of 3,000 feet, higher than any on Tutuila. Tau had no harbors, lagoons, or any suitable area for landing an amphibious plane. Big ocean swells are a menace for planes landings in the open sea. We would have preferred the smaller, choppy waters of a lagoon, harbor or river, but we had no choice. Lt. Green circled the island several times and finally decided to bring the plane down in the open ocean, several miles from what looked like the island's main beach.

The ocean was not particularly rough that day, but it did have the typical rolling swells. One had to land into the wind, crossing the swells, much like a boat navigating rough waters. This day, the height from the crest to the trough of each wave was a typical 15 feet. Ocean landings were maneuvers that should first be practiced, much like carrier landings, with which the Lt. had no previous experience. Ideally, the plan was to get the plane to stick to the water as it touched the crest of the first swell. The Lt. yelled to the crew to hang on (we used no seat belts in those days) and down we came. Sure enough we bounced off the first wave crest and found ourselves soaring some ten feet over the trough and fighting to regain lost airspeed. The Lt. then temporarily gunned the engines to stay airborne until the plane encountered the next wave crest. For a novice, he handled the situation very well, as we only ricocheted four or five times before finally sticking to the sea.

We had to taxi to the island, which seemed a few miles away. As we got within a few hundred yards of the beach, the Lt. was confronted with another dilemma. It seemed that out of nowhere there appeared a dozen or so native outrigger canoes headed straight for us. It was a welcoming committee! This presented a problem, in that we were headed straight into a group of native filled canoes, and had no way of stopping the plane as it coasted into them. These natives had never before been near an airplane and had no idea of the danger they were headed into. Applying brakes to the retracted wheels accomplished nothing. Reversing the engine props was not an available engine option in those days. The only tool left was to throw out the sea anchor aft and immediately cut the engines. Cutting the engines might make it difficult to restart them when later preparing for takeoff. The correct procedure in cutting the engines was to first rev them up and cut them while they were at high RPM. Doing this move was out of the question, as it could have dire consequences, like chewing up a slew of natives. We had no choice. The sea anchor was tossed out as the Lt. immediately cut the engines. Before we knew it, we found ourselves among the native fleet of boats. Fortunately, the plane glided forward only a few more feet, thus avoiding casualties among the approaching natives in their canoes.

When we finally stopped, we feared the very inquisitive natives would overrun the plane to get inside. The closest they had ever been to an airplane was to watch it fly several thousand feet overhead. In the past, the two sailors stationed on the island were systematically rotated every two months by replacements brought over by a small Navy boat. After much yelling and negotiating, order was finally impressed on the crowds surrounding our plane. Our pilot and a medic were whisked off in one of the canoes and headed straight for the beach. The crew was left behind to protect the plane. The fleet of canoes milled around the plane touching whatever they could to satisfy their curiosity. We young members of the crew took note of the young native girls, in that they all wore Navy tee shirts to cover their bosoms, as decreed by Navy brass. One of us posed a question: What would they look like if those tee shirts were to get soaking wet? This could be easily accomplished. We'll invite them to do a little swimming with us. So, we each emptied our pockets, stripped to the waist, chucked our shoes and dove in. We then proceeded to climb up on top of the plane's spacious wing and take turns diving into the clear blue ocean waters. It took a little coaxing to get the natives to join us, but we eventually did get our reward and were treated to seeing native girls in soaking-wet tee shirts!

After what seemed like an eternity, the shore party returned with the dying native chief, but also accompanied by two lesser chiefs. These fiercely loyal chieftains were not about to let us take away their leader unattended, and over the objections of our pilot, insisted on coming along to guard him from any harm, human or spirit. As the party was boarding, I couldn't help but notice their indescribable wide-eyed look of anxiety. After all, they were about to fly into the world of the unknown, touching perhaps, the supernatural. This was a very big bird from the sky, and they were about to take to the air to join with Mother Nature's other birds of the sky. On the other hand, our pilot was concerned that we were now somewhat over our plane's load capacity, and never having made an ocean takeoff, he became aware of the perils that might lie ahead. First, we had to sweat out getting the engines started. We needed a little luck with this maneuver. The engines should first be pulled through by hand, which is done by simply mechanically rotating the props by grasping each blade and pushing it through a rotation. This is commonly done while walking on the ground across the front of the engine. However, this maneuver could not be done at sea. It was obvious that we would have to dispense with that procedure and hope for the best. The pilot and crew held their breath as the pilot hit the starter button, cranking the engine over. This is a major drain on the battery's power. You had to get one engine started, or you could be left with dead batteries, a grim predicament to be faced with in the middle of nowhere. So the canoes were cleared away... and the moment of truth was now at hand.

Since the engines had not had time to appreciably cool, the first engine luckily started after only a few tries of cranking over. The second followed easily. In no time, we were headed for the open ocean and into the wind and swells to start our takeoff. The first thing evident to those of us on our maiden ocean takeoff, was that after many minutes into the run, we were still moving awfully slow. The reason for this is that drag, or friction, between the smooth hull, or bottom of the plane and the surface water is tremendous, thus requiring a very long takeoff path. As we headed into the swells, the props would occasionally chop into the onrushing swells, sending a heavy spray toward our tail section. We just kept going and going, with seemingly little increase in speed. After what seemed like many minutes, I'm sure most of us onboard were becoming somewhat concerned. The two native chieftains apparently sensed our apprehension. From my position in the nose of the plane, I was able to observe the anxious looks written all over their faces. After about 15 minutes, we found ourselves still riding up and down each swell, and temporarily becoming airborne between swells. Our airspeed was not enough to gain altitude, and we consequently ricocheted off the top of the next swell, lost a bit of air speed, revved the engines, and then ran into the next swell. This process seemed to repeat endlessly, and I felt at one point that the takeoff would have to be aborted. These encounters between the wave crest and the plane could eventually tear the tail section of the plane apart.

A similar scenario had ended in disaster for one of our rescue planes just a few months earlier. A new PBY, which had just arrived hours before from Hawaii as a replacement for one of the two overworked PBYs stationed at Samoa, was hurriedly dispatched to a rescue scene to pick up survivors from a downed military transport plane that had been on its way here from Hawaii. As the new PBY, loaded with crew and rescued passengers, was in its takeoff run with its props chopping into the oncoming wave crests, one of the engine's propeller blades was torn out of its hub. With the cockpit being directly in line with the arc of the rotating prop, the blade came crashing through the side of the fuselage, slicing the pilot across his body and killing him instantly. The co-pilot, Lt. Reznik, was alert enough to grab the wheel and successfully bring the plane down. A call was immediately put out for another plane to come to the rescue. At the airbase on Tutuila, the old PBY, long overdue for maintenance, was sent out to pick up the survivors of the two downed planes. Once they had all passengers safely aboard the backup PBY, the damaged new plane was left to sink.

Right after the old rescue plane with its compliment of crew and passengers landed safely on Tutuila, Lt. Reznik saw fit to make the following startling announcement: "I want to see the crew that sent out the new plane on this mission, court martialed, for failure to conduct the customary and required pre-flight inspection." Fortunately, no action by authorities followed, but Reznik instantly became very unpopular with all the enlisted men on the base.

With the present rescue mission approaching a critical stage, our young pilot managed to keep cool, stay with full throttle and finally get rewarded with a clean takeoff. The mantle of anxiety immediately lifted from the shoulders of pilot and crew, as well as from our passengers. After a relatively short trip back to Tutuila and landing at our home base without further incident, we were treated to a big surprise as we vacated our PBY and got a look at the tail assembly. The control surfaces were now in shreds! In our time, all

Navy aircraft had a skin of aluminum, but the control surfaces on the wing tips and the rudder and elevator surfaces on the tail were instead covered with a canvas type fabric. Now, we found only shreds left on these control surfaces. I'm certain Lt. Green will always remember this maiden ocean landing and takeoff, as will also the two Polynesian chieftains, whose fierce loyalty to their chief far exceeded the terror in their hearts. The old native chief did eventually recover from his wounds and happily return to his beloved Manua, but this time by boat. I'm certain a legend must still be told among his descendants on this tiny isle, a tale of their esteemed ancestor chief and his consorts, soaring high through the skies with the gods, aboard this great big Navy blue bird.

Just two days later on March 05, my autopilot services were once again needed on another PBY flight with the same pilot, Lt. Green. This time we were headed for Funafuti. This would be a five hour routine flight, not involving any high brass. The front lines had now moved well into the Marshall Islands, leaving Funafuti and the Ellice Islands in a much more relaxed state. The crew and I ate well for a change, and were privileged to a comfortable sleep indoors. The returning flight the next day turned out relaxing and uneventful. For the first time, I had the privilege of sitting in the flight engineer station, instead of my usual bombardier's place in the nose of the plane. The flight engineer's station was situated in a rather unique position and provided a much better view of the ocean seascape below than did even the pilot's position. Its location was in the five foot wide structural member that bridged the top of the cabin to the underside of the plane's massive wing, thus presenting an almost unobstructed view of the ocean below. In this windowed enclosure, the flight engineer's prime responsibility was to monitor a large array of instruments displaying the engine's performance. In most other warplanes, these instruments would have all been in direct display in the pilot's compartment. While in this perch, the engineer was also called upon to keep a sharp eye on the seascape below for enemy submarines and also for downed friendly aircraft survivors.

At this time, activities at Tafuna were definitely slowing down. Unknown to the troops, our Commanding Officer, Lt. Colonel Reisweber had lately developed serious and painful back problems. In his early career years, he had been an accomplished Marine Corps aviator, going all the way back to World War I. He had briefly left the service after that war, and went to work as a commercial pilot for a business executive. It was during this time he suffered a serious accident and was told afterwards that he would probably never walk again. He proved everyone wrong as he fully recovered and then returned to Marine Aviation duty several years later, but not as a pilot. He somehow managed his pains during the ensuing years. However, at this present time, his back pain had become unmanageable. The medical facilities at our mobile hospital strongly recommended he be immediately shipped back to the states for more effective treatment. So, the call went in to Naval Headquarters in DC to send out another ranking officer to take over the temporary command of MCAF. The existing officers presently in our group were all old salts, but none held a higher rank than that of a lieutenant.

As a commander, Colonel Reisweber was strictly military and very demanding of his troops. He kept a low profile, never directly dealing with the enlisted men. All orders were handed down through lower ranking officers. We had not known how long he had been enduring this pain, but knowing his character a bit (having spent some of my time in the office complex just outside his office), I believe he had waited until the time came when our role in supplying the war zone with airworthy planes and ammunition had become minimal before asking to be relieved of his command duties. It took about a week before our new CO arrived. The replacement turned out to be a very young major. Arrive he did, and in grand fashion, piloting a hot, new Vought F4U fighter plane, the first of its kind to land on Tutuila. He was a sight to behold, like right out of a Hollywood script, wearing designer sunglasses and a long flowing neck scarf, somewhat reminiscent of the legendary Red Baron of WW I. He had all the trappings of a hotshot and probably one of the dreaded 90-day wonders. This type seldom turned out to be a natural leader.

The Major took only a couple days to survey the situation before coming out with a stunning announcement. Since most of the rank and file men of MCAF were on Samoa for 16 months, we had all assumed that we were on the verge of being shipped back to the States in the very near future. However, the Major saw the situation in a different light. He announced that since we had it so easy during our overseas tenure in staying well behind the front lines, he would instead have us split up and reassigned to active duty with other air wings operating close to, or on nearby combat islands. Wow! This almost had the ring of being handed a punishment. But a punishment for what? Having it easy on this peaceful tropical isle, while troops further north have it rough? My guess was he wanted to come across as a tough commanding officer.

This directive didn't last for long. When our Colonel got wind of it, he immediately sent out word to all the men in our group that the proposed reassignments would not take place. He then flat out refused to turn command over to the Major, and further announced he would stay with the entire group until a way was found for all of us, as a unit, to safely return **together** to the States. Evidently, the Colonel was exercising a little practiced Navy rule stating that a Commanding Officer need not relinquish his command to his replacement, if he felt that person not fit for the command position. This standoff lasted for a week or so, and when the hot shot Major realized he wasn't winning the argument, he simply made himself very scarce.

21.   BRIEF PARADISE ON A TROPICAL ISLE

In the meantime, aircraft activity on Tutuila's base essentially came to a stop. On April 19, 1944, I was called upon to make one more final local PBY flight to fix a malfunctioning autopilot. We were now a bypassed airfield facility with few, if any, daily tasks to perform. To make life even easier, we were given only one obligation, and that was to have to answer a daily roll call. A few of our troops were still shacking up with natives in some back villages. In addition, there were now plenty of empty, choice living quarters. I found the ultimate South Sea pad in the form of a special fale, right on the lagoon's shore, and very close to the coastal surf. Now, I could enjoy being serenaded to sleep each night by the soothing sounds of the nearby gentle surf. Also our latrine-on-stilts was now only a short walk down the beach. Near to my new fale was another that housed our two "field musics," better known in other military organizations as buglers. Their nightly rendition of Taps was always a rather moving experience, especially in this lonely, remote landscape. They also kept a pet dog named Egbert, whose typical antics added a bit of joy to our daily lives.

Adding another touch of luxury to the mix, I was very fortunate during one of my daily walks along the coastline, to come across a damaged rowboat that had just washed up on the beach. It was obviously a product of a recent, nearby ship sinking. Although still in one piece, it was generally in poor shape. I had lots of time on my hands and diligently went about making it sea worthy once more. I was also very lucky in finding a pair of old oars that had been stashed deep in a corner of rarely used old storage building. Soon, I became privileged to spend many hours of each day afloat, exploring the many attractive features of the lagoon and its long shoreline. One of these features was a long, slender peninsula that projected from the mainland out toward the end of the runway, and almost to the surf line. This peninsula was called Nuuuli, or Coconut Point as dubbed by the Marines. It had on it one of the nicest villages on the entire island, and understandably held a sizable native population. It was said to have also been the filming site of an old hurricane movie about the South Pacific.

In harmony with my nightly serenade from the soothing surf, the natives held daily singing and dancing sessions late every evening. The rhythmic beat of their drums was especially entertaining. Occasionally, during the day I rowed over to their village just to wander around. They were always very cordial and friendly, but more than anything, were always a happy people.

While cruising on the water one particular day, I pulled up an old lobster pot, or trap. Out of curiosity, I wondered if I could catch anything with it. I managed to find suitable bait, and drop the pot off in deeper waters of the lagoon. When I checked it a few days later, I was amazed to find it had trapped a huge lobster, estimated to weigh about 15 pounds. Of course, it got me rather excited, but now what do I do with it? It should make a great dinner for a few chosen Marines left at the base, so I immediately ran it over to the mess hall and proudly presented it to our cooks. To my amazement, they wouldn't have anything to do with it. Our cooks were not very good at their trade, to say the least. I immediately jumped back in my boat, and rowed over to the native village with my prized catch. The native chiefs were delighted. This would fit in well with their exclusive sea food diet. There were no cattle or chicken farms on the whole island. The abundant sea food from local waters fulfilled all their protein needs. I was given a cordial invitation to attend the feast that night, but declined due to my strict reluctance in spending evenings or night times inside any of the native villages.

Meanwhile, time dragged on. We stayed on the alert for any big ships that might be cruising into the harbor. The shipping lane channel leading into the harbor conveniently passed closely along the coast directly off the airbase, and so any big ships coming in would be clearly visible to anyone at the airbase. For a few weeks we watched for ships, but the scene continued to remain barren. A feeling of being marooned started to come over us. After all, this part of the Pacific was now playing a minimal role in the war effort. Everything to and from the States, by sea or air, was now moving along the new, northerly route. The Colonel might now be having second thoughts about passing up the opportunity of getting himself back to the States, but instead chose to stick it out and stay with us. We troops surely didn't have any cause to complain about hardships. Other than the loneliness for family back home, this could become an almost idyllic way of life. I also felt that if the occasion were to arise, I might want to volunteer to stay over for a while in assisting any new crew in running the air base. I got that opportunity when on May 01, operations of activities at the MCAS at Tutuila were officially turned over to a skeleton US Navy crew. Unfortunately, my offer was succinctly declined.

Several months previous, probably due to the long, drawn out monotony, I must have lost all sense of good reasoning when I foolishly wrote a "Dear John" letter to Neshie, my ever faithful childhood sweetheart. How could I do something so cruel to someone who so least deserved it? Dear John letters commonly originated from lonely sweethearts back home, who chose to date an available local guy, so they didn't have to endure a long wait for their men to return from extended duties on the warfront. In my case, there wasn't any someone else. The native women on the island were Polynesian and somewhat attractive, but never did stir any desire for me to get involved.

But now there would be a new female about to enter my life. Her name was Helen, and she was not present here on Samoa, rather, she lived in Nanticoke, a neighboring town to my hometown of Ashley, PA. To top it all off, I had yet to meet her in person. It all started when Sophie, my older sister who also lived in Nanticoke, and who had been a very frequent letter writer to me, described Helen as a bright, attractive blonde daughter of a prominent local businessman and a family friend. Sophie had strong aspirations for being a matchmaker. In a flood of mail, she told me what a beauty Helen was and that we could have so much fun together, this even though I had never previously voiced any doubts about staying with my Neshie. She then got Helen to start writing chummy and enticing letters to me, like "I'm so anxious for you to get here. We could take long canoe rides on the lake at night, and have the cottage all to ourselves all night…" And her family did own a cottage on a popular nearby lake. I hate admitting to falling for this typical call of the siren bait, but I did. And it wasn't long afterwards that I made the inexcusable choice of writing that Dear John letter to my sweetheart, saying that I needed time to think things over, and take time to shop around before committing to any permanent relationship. I can only offer that I was probably going through some period of depression due to the long preceding loneliness on our island.

When my Dear John letter reached my sweetheart Neshie back home, it must have devastated her. She worked in her father's grocery store, located in the front section of their big home. My Mom was one of the store's regular customers and she and Neshie often warmly greeted each other in the store. The day after Neshie received the letter, she was on duty in the store when my Mom walked in and cordially greeted her. However, my sweetheart didn't respond, but instead burst into tears and promptly bolted out of the store and into the attached house. My Mom immediately saw that something was radically wrong, but being from the old country she knew she would need help in unraveling this mystery. So she promptly walked over to the close-by residence of my other sister, Jennie, and asked her to look into the matter. I had spent much of my early years at Jennie's home, and was quite close to her. She was a good soul and was liked by everyone, especially by Neshie. That evening, she took my heartbroken sweetheart for a long walk and dragged the whole sad story out of her. I can only imagine the conversation between the two, but I did later find out that Jennie stressed to not give up on me, that I must be all mixed up, to keep writing, and to wait until I returned home on leave. Then at that time, she should take on a more aggressive attitude toward hanging onto me.

Back on Tutuila, what we had been waiting for finally did happen one day as a very big ship appeared, cruising across our line of sight, and heading right down the channel leading into the harbor. The Colonel was promptly alerted, and accompanied by few of his top officers, immediately headed for Pago Pago. This was it! Presumptuously, all the men started packing their duds in preparation for a quick departure off the island. However, news soon drifted back that things at the docks were not all peaches and cream. Our Colonel was to learn that this ship, the SS Republic, a luxury liner converted into a troop ship, had recently delivered 3,000 troops for the Hollandia invasion off the coast of New Guinea. During the battle, the ship ran aground and suffered serious structural damage, leading to daily recurrences of onboard electrical fires. This condition made it necessary to ban any future carrying of passengers. The ship sorely needed major repairs done at the Navy base in San Francisco, but would first need temporary repairs done at Pearl Harbor along the way. The ship's Captain would not consider taking on any additional passengers. On this, he was adamant. However, our Colonel, stuck to his guns, and pleaded that since we were such a small group we should not pose any further burden. Our numbers had dwindled down to less than 100 men after having lost many that had been sent back to the States during the filariasis epidemic. The Colonel also argued that we were becoming desperate in finding transportation to the States, and were willing to take our chances. The ship's Captain did finally accede. We were given a couple days to get packed and ready.

Pearl Harbor! Oh boy, will this be a real treat! Most troops that served in the Pacific theater had the pleasure of a stopover and liberty in Hawaii, and none ever had a bad word to say about it. As with most other Marines at the airbase, I didn't have much to pack. Our original uniforms had long ago been discarded due to mold. Souvenirs were scarce and few available. However, I did have a large and rather unusual item that needed attention, and that was my restored rowboat. I sure did have lots of fun with it during the past few relaxing weeks. One experience was worth recounting, involving a visiting SBD dive bomber. The reason for this visit did not involve my services. However, a few hours later during its subsequent takeoff, the plane uncontrollably drifted off the side of the runway, and crashed into the waters of the shallow lagoon. It was not a destructive crash, more like a vehicle crash. The pilot was not hurt and simply crawled out, able to walk over the submerged bed of coral to climb up and onto the runway.

Subsequent recovery efforts all proved futile. Normally, a special crash boat would have been dispatched to the site to winch the crashed aircraft up and onto a floating barge. However, in this case, that would not be possible since the waters were quite shallow with outcroppings of coral that would have prevented the rescue craft from reaching its target. A new approach was tried. A tow truck with winch, hook and cable was summoned and positioned on the side of the runway nearest to the stricken plane. Efforts in trying to toss the hook and cable to the plane all proved futile. The hardware was just too heavy and cumbersome to be carried by hand. Up to this point, I had hung around in my rowboat, casually observing these failed attempts. Finally, I stepped in to offer a guarded suggestion: "How about using my boat to get the heavy hook and cable out to the plane? I could try rowing it out to the plane." The distance to the plane was about 30 feet. To my surprise, they decided to give it a try. The weight of the hook and resistance of the cable still attached to the truck proved to be almost overwhelming, but I did ultimately succeed in oaring the hook over to the partially submerged plane, where a couple of waiting Navy divers were able to attach it to the plane. The winch then simply dragged the helpless plane across the coral, and then hauled it up and onto the runway. In the process, the poor SBD might as well have suffered a real crash landing for all the damage that was sustained as a result of this unorthodox rescue operation.

Afterwards, I felt pretty good about my role in this operation. So much so, that I had the gall to approach Navy brass at Pago Pago and ask they consider commissioning my boat as a true Navy rescue vessel. Of course, my request was curtly greeted with a dash of derision. After this, I still had to find a new home for my now famed sea craft. So, I spread the word around that it was for sale with a price tag of $200. The very first inquiry came from a totally unexpected source, the American Red Cross, but why would they be interested? The Red Cross did make their presence known throughout most overseas military bases, but on Samoa it seemed only to assure that we troops enjoyed a constant supply of cheap cigarettes. We had infrequent old movies, absolutely no recreational equipment, almost nothing tangible for entertainment. Maybe they served a more meaningful purpose wherever natural disasters took place, but on Tutuila, they acted like they were on vacation. I was firmly told that since this boat was now situated at a military base, it was considered Navy property and as such, a recreational item with its use to be turned over to and administered by the Red Cross. I didn't hesitate in answering that it was my property, and mine alone, and that I was going to sell it, and if they didn't like it, they could "Go to Hell." My coarse utterance brought out a menacing reply from the officer behind the desk: "This kind of talk can get you court martialed." "Go to Hell" was my instant reiteration. With a final "Go to Hell," I stomped out of the room. I am quite happy to report that in the end, the Red Cross did not pursue the matter any further, and that ultimately, an incoming sailor showed a strong desire to own the boat. I was happy to hand it over to him for a mere hundred bucks.

22. THE VOYAGE HOME

On May 16, 1944, the remnant troops and officers of Marine Corps Air Facility at the Tafuna airbase on Tutuila, American Samoa, happily boarded the converted troop ship, the SS Republic, and without any native farewells, sailed from their tropical paradise home of 17 months, heading straight for Pearl Harbor. This journey would be full of hope, but perhaps not free of perils. As per Navy wartime practice, we were required to spend each day's dusk and dawn hours in assembly topside on the open decks while the ship assumed a prescribed zig zag course. This practice was meant to present a difficult target for any enemy sub that might be stalking us. This twice daily ritual was conducted in an almost military style by our overly regulation-zealous First Sargent. He proceeded to add to the inconvenience by ordering all troops to stand at a loose attention during the entire time on the deck. This act could last more than an hour. And, believe it or not, the equator at dawn could be a very cold place. I personally remember feeling the chills. There was absolutely no reason for us not to be allowed to move around while on deck to help ward off boredom and stay warm. The reason, he claimed, for keeping us in a tight formation was for our own safety: to facilitate a rapid abandonment of ship were we to be fatally torpedoed. Our First Sarge surely earned the dubious distinction of being a real chicken shit NCO. He was universally disliked by all the troops.

It wasn't long before we found ourselves about to cross the Equator. As discussed earlier, Navy tradition dictated that all passengers were obliged to endure the customary initiation for their first-time-crossing of the Equator. We had been spared this ritual on our westward passage over the Equator 17 months earlier, because all aboard were so busy paying attention to the stalking enemy submarine on our tail. We had heard that these initiation practices could be rather unpleasant, but that didn't turn out to be the case after all. I suppose that since we were such a small, inconspicuous bunch, we just did not merit the time for the serious dispensations of Navy traditions. Instead, we simply were issued small aqua colored, official looking business cards, signed by a couple of our officers as "Davy Jones" and "Neptunus Rex", attesting that, in 1944, we had officially crossed the Equator.

On the good side, there was lots of leisure time to while away. It was a huge ship and we passengers totaled only about 100, whereas this ship had just recently transported 3,000 Army troops to the battle area. We now had all the room we needed, great sleeping quarters, lots of fresh water, great Navy chow and lots of lively games of chance to enjoy. The Navy crew aboard had a field day fleecing the previous naïve passengers heading for the battle zones. We found the Navy crew lush with their winnings, but somewhat reluctant to take on us card playing veterans. They may have also sensed that few of us were carrying any appreciable amount of cash. Eventually, their reluctance faded, and succumbing to the powers of greed, they took us on. Soon there were many groups of troops entranced in the popular card games of black jack and poker. I was among the ones with very little cash on hand, in fact only having $5.00 in my pocket when we boarded. Borrowing money was not an easy task, since nobody in our group carried any reasonable amount of cash.

However, I felt I had to participate in some way or another with my paltry $5.00. I smartened up by joining a small group playing Hearts, which by most money standards was considered a sissy game. But, in this game, one could play very conservatively with small bets and make his money last. I hit a hot streak right off the bat and ran my $5.00 up to $20.00. With that cushion of cash, I immediately jumped into the nearest poker gathering. My hot streak continued for the first day, and I ran my winnings up to near $1,000. Wow! However, on the following day, my luck went into reverse as I watched my winnings rapidly dwindle. Since I was never the greedy one, I stopped playing when I got down to $200, at which time I promptly loaned out most of it to some eager friends in need. I felt sure of being reimbursed soon after landing in the States. I kept just enough for a Hawaii liberty. I was now able to sit back and enjoy the rest of this pleasure cruise on our way to Hawaii.

A few small islands existed along the route where we could take refuge in case of an extreme emergency. However, as we approached Pearl, the frequency of on-board fires started to diminish, and subsequently ceased entirely. The ship's Captain then made the snap decision to change course and head straight for San Francisco. Most of us were a bit disappointed since Pearl was the ultimate liberty town for servicemen. However, getting back to 'Frisco' sooner than expected might even be a better bet.

The mood of anticipation increased daily as we drew nearer and nearer to the American coastline. What would life be like back in the civilized world? Surely, there should be no traces of malaria, filariasis or body-consuming fungus here in the States, right? Are those big holidays still being celebrated? We had just spent two Christmases and two Easters far, far from home. Would we continue to have powdered eggs for breakfast, dehydrated potatoes and mutton for dinner? Is there still such a thing as a nice, juicy steak? Are there still friendly slop shutes around where one could sit down with a few of his buddies, trade stories and down a few rounds of good beer? Are there still movies to see and radio stations that fill the air? And most of all, what will it feel like to hold your sweetheart in your arms for real, and not just in your dreams? (Although, on this last question, I knew I would be walking into a big turmoil after having sent home that Dear John letter.)

Finally one day, the word came through that the mainland lay just over the horizon. The excitement then really started to mount. Then it occurred to me that there would likely be a greeting party at the docks and that I was not looking very presentable. This prompted me to dash below, do a quick shave and shower and find some decent clothes to wear. I raced through all those moves, convinced I had time to spare, but when I dashed back up topside I was devastated to observe the outline of the famed Golden Gate Bridge, rapidly fading away in our wake! We already had passed under it! I did it again! I had previously missed this privilege on our voyage out of San Francisco 18 months earlier, but that was through no fault of my own, since without announcement, that ship made sail in the middle of the night. But the disappointment was soon to fade as we pulled up to a spacious dock. A diagonal parallel stair ramp was put in place for us to disembark. There was no cheering crowd, only the smiling faces of many volunteer workers offering us their warm greetings. After all, we weren't exactly a boatload of heroes. As we filtered down the gangplank, a Red Cross worker jumped out of the line of greeters to assist one of us who happened to be on crutches. He was our unit's parachute packer, a rather solitary assignment. Recently, at work, he had fallen off a stool and fractured his leg. Not exactly a war wound. Nevertheless, he was afforded a hero's welcome. Of course, our clumsy hero later took a good ribbing from his buddies.

The entire group was then funneled into a sheltered outdoor eating area and promptly served a breakfast of REAL bacon and FRESH eggs. The flavor of that simple meal will be forever etched in my mind. As soon as the meal was over, we were mustered to receive a surprise announcement from the old man (our CO), very likely wanting to wish us a final fond farewell. All enlisted men returning from overseas duty were required to report to a clearing center, go on furlough and then wait for orders for transfer to a new base. The commissioned officers had already received their new assignments and were obligated to proceed directly to their new bases. We realized it would be our last time together with this family of officers. We really didn't know quite what to expect from our CO. He was somewhat of a mystery to the enlisted men, with his aloofness and firmness of command. But his choosing to spend several months enduring extreme pain when he could have been comfortably treated at a stateside hospital, left us wondering: What was he made of?... What could he possibly want to say to us?

The gathered enlisted men quietly waited for his words. Colonel Reisweber started by simply telling of being very proud of us, and that he was indeed fortunate to have served with us. But as he went on, words started to fail him and emotion slowly took over. Eventually, he found himself too choked up to continue, stood silent for a few moments and then just simply walked away. We were dumbfounded! This guy was human after all! We never anticipated this to happen and were deeply moved by his display of emotion. This man was indeed a true leader. He did not have to lead us on a cavalry charge or on a dangerous beach assault. Instead he took on a daring, secret overseas assignment, which after a short while turned into a mediocre one, but he did successfully get that job done. More important, while enduring much pain, he sacrificed himself by staying with his men and assuring their safe return to the States. I'm sure all have remembered his sacrifice and the devotion he exhibited to the men under his charge.

The date is May 30, 1944.

WELCOME HOME, MARINES.
GOOD SHOW!

Even though few of us had fresh uniforms on hand and few had spending money, we all did enjoy one brief liberty in "Frisco." Then unceremoniously, off to San Diego we headed early the next day. The huge Marine Camp at Miramar was our destination and would be our home for a month or two while waiting for our much anticipated 30 day furloughs, and then for assignments to new bases.

PART 4 - FURLOUGHS, FLYING AND FUN

23.   THE LONG AWAITED 30 DAY FURLOUGH

Upon arrival at Camp Miramar on June 1, 1944, I seemed happy, but was not in very good physical shape, still feeling the effects of coming down with the chills while aboard ship, but more than that, in finding myself somewhat depressed over messing up my relationship with my sweetheart back home. At Miramar, we lolled around for a couple of weeks getting issued new clothes and just getting squared away. I got to feeling worse physically as the days dragged by. I didn't even feel much like going on liberty in San Diego. My buddies, on the other hand were making up for the long time spent away from civilization by whooping it up every night, getting tanked and finding pleasurable female companionship. Finally, on June 16, the much earned 30 day overseas furloughs were issued to all.

The train ride home would be a long and uncomfortable one, especially since there would be no Pullman car in which to spend the nights. It meant sitting and sleeping in the same seat for four or five nights, and the train was dirty. There was nothing to do except wallow in discomfort and feel sorry for myself, even though I was headed for home and should be in great spirits. In switching trains in Chicago for the last day's leg of the journey, I found myself aboard a train that was even more dirty and grimy, making me feel even lousier. Finally, I couldn't take the misery anymore, so I decided to leave the train at Harrisburg, PA and grab a bus headed for Wilkes-Barre. It actually saved me a little time, because I would have had to change trains at Philadelphia to reach my final rail destination in Wilkes-Barre. And the bus ride turned out to be rather scenic and more comfortable.

The bus terminal at Wilkes-Barre was situated near the city's Square, a name given because all of its major roads converged at that point. I eagerly entered the Square and immediately started looking for the road that would lead me out toward my home town of Ashley, some four miles away. I walked around the Square a few times only to find that I wasn't able to recognize any of the outgoing streets.

Nothing looked familiar. Just two years previous, while attending college courses at a local institution, I had spent my daily lunch breaks relaxing in the town's square. Now, it all looked so strange to me. The situation was starting to become unnerving. How could this happen? Sure, I was physically pretty sick and somewhat depressed, but was I also losing my mind? Taking a guess, I picked one particular street and proceeded to follow it away from the center of town. As I walked along, things started to look more and more familiar. Eventually, I knew I was headed for home and was then able to hitch a ride the rest of the way. When I got to my home street, I found it also to look a bit unfamiliar. Finally, after a long, two year absence, this now 19 year old veteran Marine found himself entering his family home and being lovingly greeted by his aged parents, grateful to have their baby son home from the war.

After taking time to assess my poor physical health, Mom insisted that I immediately see a doctor. It was a weekend, but our devoted family physician, Dr. Joe Doherty, never refused to see a needy patient, no matter the time or day of the week. He soon determined that I had fluid in or around my lungs, as in the case of pleurisy. His recommendation was to have it drained, but this procedure would require hospitalization. I explained that my time was limited and that I wished to be with family and loved ones for the remainder of this long awaited furlough. Consequently, he prescribed medication which included a painkiller and told me to take it real easy during the rest of my leave.

Up to this time, I had not as yet paid a visit to Neshie, my sweetheart. Mindlessly, I had allowed myself to be put into a situation whereby I wasn't sure I still had a sweetheart and that I might be seeing someone entirely new while on furlough, and possibly from now on. My sister Sophie, who had originally steered me into corresponding with another girl, unbeknownst to me had organized a welcome home party of relatives and friends, which was to be held at her home in Nanticoke. There, I was to be formally introduced to Helen, the new female who recently had been thrust into my life. However, my very wise and compassionate other sister Jennie, caught wind of the party scheme and promptly stepped in and convinced Neshie to come to the party, even though neither had been invited. Her plan was to stay at my sweetheart's side and also to see that I would not be capitalized by the new woman. Apparently, Jennie had told Neshie to pick out her best and brightest dress, and to come over to her house to get dolled up before the party. Neshie panicked, realizing that she had nothing to wear - no nice dress. Again, Jennie came to the rescue and somehow found a perfect fitting, bright-colored dress for my sweetheart. The afternoon of the party, Neshie got cleaned up, and with Jennie's help, did her hair and put on just the right amount of make-up, resulting in a beauty to surely catch my eye. On the evening of the party, Jennie did accompany Neshie, and impressed upon her that on finally meeting me there, she should firmly latch onto my arm and not let go. At that fateful moment, Jennie saw to it that this actually took place, sending Neshie straight in my direction. Sure enough, Neshie latched onto my arm the instant we met, and I was re-captured. Sophie wasn't happy to find Neshie present at the party, but was left no choice, since I was the guest of honor and displayed being thrilled to once again have my sweetheart stuck at my side.

My Sweetheart, Neshie, 1941

When Helen, the other guest of honor, arrived and was introduced to me, she was astonished in finding Neshie firmly and permanently wrapped around my arm. After a formal exchange of niceties amongst all, the situation settled down to routine chatter. I now belonged to the only true love in my life, the same one I had departed from almost three years prior, as a test of forced absence, a test of our youthful devotion to each other. Jennie's simple plan had saved the day for us. In what seemed like a miracle, I suddenly felt free from the depression I had been experiencing for the past few months. Deep inside, I once more felt like a very happy person. Unfortunately, I do not recall apologizing for my poor judgment and for the unnecessary grief I had caused my sweetheart. The subject was never brought up again throughout our whole lifetime together of 67 years, a tribute to Neshie's selfless character. We spent the rest of my furlough together each day and evening in what felt like total bliss. And, magically, my health once again slowly became restored. Now, our only enemy was the clock. We only had about two weeks left to spend together and to dream of our bright future ahead. I still had two more years to serve in the military, but with the outcome of the war now looking very favorable for our nation, we could entertain optimistic dreams of spending a happy life together forever.

The return trip to California would differ immensely from the one that just brought me home. The train ride to Chicago turned out to be comfortable, pleasant and uneventful. In Chicago, I was lucky to get aboard the rail line's touted express train, the Super Chief. Unfortunately, as before, there were no Pullman cars available and so all passengers were left to find a comfortable way to sleep while confined to their seats. From there, the trip turned out to be quite eventful. When the train was not too far across the state of Illinois, I ran into another Marine, somewhat younger than I was. He, too, had been overseas for a while and seemed to find pleasure in recounting to other passengers some of his personal experiences. But when he started showing pictures of natives suffering from dreadful tropical diseases, I decided I had heard enough. I took him aside, thoroughly reprimanding him, explaining that as a Marine, what he was doing was disgraceful. This was no place for him to carry on with such grandstanding. As a senior NCO, I felt it my duty to set him straight. I was relieved to see him not put up an argument and afterwards to behave more civilly.

Also boarding the train in St. Louis, MO was a young mother tending to a small boy. As she entered the car and looked about, she displayed a look of concern, presumably at seeing the lack of comfortable quarters. After watching her struggle to find a comfortable seat for herself and her young son, I suddenly felt compelled to step in and offer assistance. I introduced myself and offered to help in any way. With a trace of uneasiness, she allowed me to sit with them. She too, was headed for California, and was to join her husband who was an Army NCO stationed at a military base at Long Beach, CA, just outside of Los Angeles. Her name was Mary Ellen. She was about 23 years of age, and her boy about 16 months old. He was an active and tough looking boy, and could be a real handful to manage during a long, three day journey while confined aboard an ordinary railroad passenger car. Mary Ellen seemed a bit reluctant in accepting my help, perhaps because of my being a young serviceman. But, she did let me freely handle the little guy, who I appropriately named Butch, and we bonded almost immediately. Her suspicions of me slowly faded away as I tended to Butch on an almost constant basis. The train was rather crowded at the time, but there were some empty seats scattered about. I talked a few people into moving so that we could have four seats to ourselves. The backs of the seats were movable, so that instead of their being in tandem, we could have two opposing seats face each other so that Butch could have the one seat entirely to himself to play on, and much more importantly, to sleep on. And we, his guardians, could sit facing him, having our knees placed against his seat, thus keeping him safely confined.

Gradually, this little family became a fixture in our car. We made frequent trips together to the dining car, with me tending to Butch as if he were my own. I became a good influence when it came to getting him to eat and allowing his mother to enjoy her meal, or when she needed time for personal reasons. Passengers eventually assumed that I was his daddy. Butch was a handful because he was so active. After just the first day, there was little doubt that Mary Ellen would have had a tough trip if she had to do this all alone. The first night brought about some doubts as to whether Butch would sleep well under the circumstances and also whether his mother could do likewise. His makeshift bench bed was rather firm, but turned out to be very practical. Surprisingly, Mary Ellen slept very well the first night. She must have been exhausted. In trying to find a comfortable position to sleep in while sitting, she would unintentionally lean her head on my shoulder and then fall fast asleep. I managed to keep my eye on Butch by staying mostly awake, catching only short cat-naps. Then the next morning this little "family" would scamper off to the dining car for breakfast. By this time I started feeling rather good about myself and life in general. There no longer existed any room for doom and gloom. Life was great once more.

In the meantime, one other passenger had been taking interest in this entertaining scene. He had earlier witnessed my reprimand of the loose-mouthed young Marine and later approached and asked to have a chat with me. Much to my surprise, he revealed himself as a Baptist minister. What could he possibly have to say to me? First, he commended the way I had handled the indiscreet young Marine. He then followed by praising the way I had assumed the fatherly duties with Butch and his mother. With many questions he then started to delve deeply into my background and my personal life. His style of interrogation left me rather uneasy. He possessed steel blues eyes, and when he looked and talked, it felt like he was seeing right through me. It was almost disturbing. When I told him I was not the boy's Dad, he really perked up. This is when he revealed that as a Baptist minister, he was associated with a seminary in Kansas City. He admitted that it was one of his duties to periodically ride the train in search for future candidates for the Baptists' ministry.

I explained that I was happy as a Catholic. This did not seem to matter to him. Evidently, his intense probing convinced him that I would make a good Baptist minister. He must have felt that my Catholic faith was not very deep, and lauded over how I had handled matters while on the train. He felt that I possessed the kind of qualities he was seeking. I was rather flabbergasted to have this sort of praise bestowed upon me, but told him I didn't feel that I could possibly fit into this radically new path in life and that I would need to have lots of time to ponder the proposition. He had no problem with that, and followed by leaving me his calling card. As he departed from the train the next day, I did get the chance to have a few brief parting words with him and again be on the receiving end of a final, deep, penetrating gaze from him.

Meanwhile, life with Butch and Mary Ellen now proceeded with a much clearer purpose. We were indeed one happy family with Butch and I acting the part of a typical American dad and son, but with Mary Ellen still a bit uneasy about my temporary role as head of the family. The second night was somewhat memorable. Mary Ellen stayed awake much longer, but now also acted much more content, and would occasionally break into singing a soft slumber song to her little boy in order to get him to fall asleep. She carried a beautiful singing voice. She then admitted that she had occasionally been a professional singer at certain night clubs. I hadn't noticed before, but now in taking a good look at her, I realized that she was indeed very pretty. The third night found her completely at ease with my close presence. While trying to fall asleep, she seemed to find much comfort in snuggling as we sat together with her head on my shoulder. Earlier that evening, she startled me as she looked deep into my eyes and said: "If only I had met you when I was 19 or 20 years old." I didn't quite know what to make of that, but found it a bit disturbing. I had, at no time, ever entertained any thought of making a pass at her, and now, certainly did not wish to lead her on. I wisely changed the subject.

While still harboring good thoughts about my presence, she suddenly came up with the idea that I must meet her husband. She insisted that sometime soon after our arrivals in California, I come up from San Diego and pay a short visit to her little family. I didn't quite go for the idea, since it would put me in an uncomfortable position, knowing that Mary Ellen would tell her husband all the good things I had done for her and her precious little boy. I much feared he would instinctively doubt that my intentions had been totally honorable. And so, the rest of the trip passed quickly and ended as Mary Ellen and Butch gave their farewells at the Los Angeles station and I continued on to San Diego. I was able to pay that visit to Long Beach several weeks later and met her husband, the real father of my recently adopted family. We spent only a few hours together, and my previous fears proved to be correct as I noted his intense glare as he spoke to me, indicating his distrust. This look and display of distrust remained throughout the entire encounter, spoiling the atmosphere of this anticipated meeting. In the end, I was glad when it came time for me to leave. Butch and his pretty Momma would now become a simple but cherished memory tucked away in the deep recesses of my mind.

July 23, 1944 found me back at Camp Miramar, California to learn the location of my new assignment. Typically, enlisted men returning from overseas would be sent to an area where they could experience light duty, rest and relaxation. A trade school would fit the bill for most. At this time, I found that they had me listed to attend Naval Bombsight School at NAS in Jacksonville, FL. There was only one thing wrong with this assignment: I had already completed Bombsight School in the summer of 1942, at the Naval Proving Grounds in Dahlgren, VA. I asked if Jacksonville was an advanced school. No, I was told, this was the same school. It turns out that during my absence of 22 months, the school had been moved from VA to FL. I informed the Miramar authorities that I had already attended Bombsight School, had been an experienced bombsight mechanic overseas for the last 17 months, and therefore did not wish to do it again. They insisted, saying I might learn something new, since it was in a different place. Once again, I outright refused, saying that I considered it a waste of time. They then threatened me with court martial if I didn't accede. I told them "Go ahead, I don't give a shit, but I am not going to Bombsight School a second time. It shouldn't be so hard to find different trade school for me!"

With this impasse, I languished at Miramar for several weeks. All my overseas buddies had already shipped out to their new posts. I had nothing to do except answer to a daily roster. I still didn't feel like whooping it up with nightly liberty in nearby San Diego. Finally, I was handed a brief assignment. Camp Miramar was a sprawling Marine Corps base that also contained a big airfield, accommodating big multi-engine bombers. There was a lot of air traffic over the entire base. Before my furlough one day, I was lined up on the parade grounds with a group of my comrades watching a flight of bombers fly low over the grounds, and heading for the landing field just a mile or so away from the grounds. As we watched each bomber, one by one, disappear behind a stand of tall trees and land on a runway, a tremendous explosion, accompanied by a fireball took place over the obscured field. We then heard the faint sounds from a flurry of sirens from emergency vehicles rushing to the scene. We were later to learn that the disaster scene was much starker than first imagined. The bomber didn't crash on the runway, but instead plowed into a multi-level barracks near the field. Scuttlebutt had it that somewhere in the vicinity of 200 Marines were killed or injured.

This brief assignment handed me here was to service a faulty autopilot on one of many attack bombers lined up along a parking apron. Being a now-seasoned autopilot technician, I immediately recognized the problem and knew the solution. All I needed was a clean cloth and some good cleaning fluid. Before I was let loose to perform my task, I was obligated to read some recent Naval aircraft maintenance bulletins. Overseas, my past choice of cleaning fluid was always the popular chemical, carbon tetrachloride, or better known as carbon tet. However, Navy medical science had recently declared it to be a dangerous substance for humans to handle and banned its further use. The bulletin did not state the actual reason for banning carbon tet. I found out much later that contact with the fluid or its vapors was highly toxic to a person's liver, especially if that person were to have traces of alcohol (as with drinking lots of beer the night before) in his blood. The Navy's substitute choice of cleaning fluid was pure unleaded gasoline, such as used in lanterns. I was appalled on hearing the Navy would make such a choice. As everyone knows, gasoline is highly flammable, and to use it in the confined space in the nose of a big aircraft, one that might already be loaded with bombs and also in close proximity with dozens more identical aircraft would be ludicrous. I asked around whether there was a secondary choice, and was told there was not. Knowing that using gasoline could result in a fire and possible disaster, I made the obvious choice of going back to the reliable carbon tet. After all, I had used it extensively overseas without experiencing a problem. Fortunately, during that time there were few occasions where I had the opportunity for consuming any alcohol.

The maintenance crew at Miramar didn't care one way or the other, what I used and didn't try to stop me. After all, it was my neck, not theirs. I performed the task, but not without some trepidation. It was hot that day in southern California, and I was not familiar with this type of bomber. In my PBY's overseas autopilot repairs, I was always able to open a direct overhead hatch and provide some reasonable air ventilation. I wasn't able to do this on the bomber at Miramar. Even though I didn't linger at this task, I found myself on the verge of passing out as I neared finishing. I'm not sure whether it was from the fumes or the confined, intense heat, or a combination of both. Had I known ahead of time of the excessive heat and confinement, I may have opted differently in my choice of cleaning fluid. Fortunately in my career, I never again was required to service a malfunctioning autopilot.

24. MCAS, SANTA BARBARA

Finally, the decision on my new assignment came through. On September 02, 1944, I would be sent to the Marine Corps Air Station in Santa Barbara, CA as part of Headquarters Squadron MAG 42. This air base, just 100 miles north of Los Angeles, sat on a high bluff overlooking the Pacific Ocean. It was built on land leased from the University of California which afterwards continued to conduct some of its classes there. In the 1930s, it was first used by a commercial airline, then in 1942, the Marines took over the airfield to use it primarily for training Marine pilots and aerial gunners. Ultimately it would become the center for training and administering Marine carrier air groups.

The base did not have the customary slop shute, but just outside the main gate, sat a small local bar and a great place to spend evenings. Technically, the airport sat in the town of Goleta, and was smirkly dubbed "Goletacanal", to make it sound like the famous Guadalcanal. The principal bartender there was a classic! His name was "Abie", and he was from New York City. He loved the Marines and the Marines loved him. He loved to entertain the troops by using bird calls and hand gestures. Unlike in San Diego, here in Goleta, underage Marines had little problem buying a drink, nor in the big town of Santa Barbara, which was a delightful place to spend long-evening liberties. The town's population was very friendly to servicemen and always kept its streets squeaky clean.

For a brief time I did the run of the mill ordnance maintenance on Marine fighter, torpedo and dive bomber planes. One day I was called in and given a rather unusual assignment. Lately, the air base had been under close scrutiny by Federal officials in trying to stop rampant smuggling of some prime foods, as well as weapons, from the base. The loss of service rifles and handguns was of great concern. To put a stop to this brazen pilfering, a plan was devised to have all resident servicemen temporarily relieved of their weapons, all of which would then be stored and guarded in a building on a remote section of the airbase. If and when a serviceman had need of his rifle, such as for a parade or scheduled rifle practice, he would be required to visit this building and check out his weapon that was stored there, and return it immediately after finishing with its intended use. A very close record would be kept of all these transactions. I was assigned to operate this facility, and be assisted by "Red", another South Pacific veteran, and native of upstate NY. The remote shack we occupied would also be our home. It was old, crude and dilapidated. It had a makeshift heating device which we were reluctant to use except when the typical coastal temperatures turned cool for the night. Furniture was crude. It was not a cozy place to spend our days and nights. One of us always had to be there on duty. Liberty in town for us was temporarily suspended. You might say we were considered under quarantine. But we were lucky to have electricity. Except for visiting the chow hall, we had just one human contact within the base and the outside world. His name was Pfeiffer. He always wore a plain Marine uniform, which showed no visible rank. Red and I were sure he was FBI, but were never clever enough to get him to admit it. His orders were always sharp and direct, although never condescending. To make him even more unapproachable, he often brought along his pet monkey, always content to perch on anyone's shoulder.

Kelly and Pfeiffer   Pfeiffer's pet monkey

The operation ran smoothly week after week. But it did get lonely out on this remote section of the airfield. Red was not what you would call an ideal partner. He finished a long tour of duty in the tropics of New Guinea and unfortunately contracted a bad case of body fungus. His affliction was somewhat severe. He complained constantly and held the government accountable for his misery. However, Red was not very clean about himself, and didn't seem to care if the fungus ran rampant. All South Pacific veterans suffered with fungus to some degree, but we tried to handle the affliction best as we could and move on with our lives.

Evenings were especially trying. Having camaraderie with the usual gang was missed. We only had each other. And our personalities couldn't have been any more unalike. Red was kind of crude in his talk and ways. One day, he somehow mustered up a portable record player. His choice of entertaining music was Cab Callaway's LP recording of "Minnie the Moocher." After putting up with countless playings of this one and only album, I was able to talk Pfeiffer into helping me get a set of classical music records. It then took a while for Red and me to resolve who was to have the LP player for a particular evening.

After a few weeks, the sting was over and the criminals apprehended. As usual, Red and I were given no further details. However, we were ecstatic to later learn that we were both to be rewarded with 15 day furloughs for our sacrifice and successful fulfillment of the assignment. Further, Pfeiffer made commercial flight arrangements for each of us to be flown to our homes on the East Coast and back. A train ride would have typically used up eight to nine days. So, here I was, on November 17, once more on my way home only four months after my overseas furlough. This time no personal or dramatic events would take place, only a happy two weeks with my parents and my precious sweetheart. Just what a furlough ought to be.

In January of 1945, word came out that our whole air group at Santa Barbara was being shipped overseas. Further, the group was being assigned to an aircraft carrier as part of a new Navy task force with plans for delivering effective air strikes to the mainland of southern Japan. Now here is where my past was going to save me from an uncertain future. As far as I knew, I was the only Marine in the group who had already done a tour of overseas duty. My being stationed in Santa Barbara was a direct result of my own making, that is, in refusing to take a transfer to Bombsight School in Jacksonville, FL several months ago. What do I do now? I only have myself to blame, but do not wish to take on airs of a crybaby, so I decided not to contest being shipped overseas a second time. However, soon after, I was somewhat relieved to learn that someone in the office found that my records showed I had not been back in the States for very long. They made the decision to leave me behind, and would now have to find a new assignment for me. The base at Santa Barbara then became barren in mid-January, with little for me to do except wait for a new assignment.

I could have started doing serious liberty every night, but somehow boozing still did not seem very appealing to me. I had not as yet mastered the art of holding my liquor, but it was still fun to hit the town and watch my buddies get pie-eyed. The gang would always welcome me on their liberty, since they could count on returning to base with at least one clear headed Marine. I did enjoy frequent visits to Abie's bar just outside the base. By chance, I happened across a few more Marines who also had been marooned by our air group's sudden departure. We collectively decided to start attending classes at the University of California's Santa Barbara site, which was right on our airbase grounds. There were about eight of us who signed up for a course in Electrical Engineering. Our instructor, who we called Harry, happened to be one of the engineering architects used in the construction of the famous Hoover Dam. I must admit that none of us were really very avid about the complexity of a college-level electrical engineering course, as opposed to the usual trade school. We were seasoned Marines, not collegians. The service schools we had already attended were pushovers, having had no elective subjects, but only what was available through military trade schools. But, in attending university classes, we found the learning process quite different and difficult. There was a lot to learn in the related subject matter, which was very dry to this group of old salts. We would systematically steer Harry off the hard subject of engineering and ask him to tell us about all the logistical problems he had encountered in the planning and building process of the gigantic Hoover Dam. He loved this distraction and excuse to go off subject! Even though we lacked enthusiasm, we still hoped to learn something beneficial from the course. These sessions proved to be real R&R for all of us, and maybe even a bit for Harry.

25. MCAS, EL CENTRO, AND THE DESERT

After attending only three or four sessions of the electrical engineering course, my new base assignment came through. Consequently, I stopped attending classes, but didn't get around to notifying the school that I was dropping out and the reason why. On January 27, 1945, I found myself headed for the MCAS at El Centro, located deep in the Imperial Valley of southeastern CA. Surprisingly, my new outfit turned out to be Hdqtrs Squadron 42, MAG 42, a part of the same outfit I was leaving in Santa Barbara. It was now designated as (Marine Base Defense) MBDMAG-42.

This desolate region was situated in a very remote desert area about 100 miles due east of San Diego. The tiny and grimy town of El Centro proved to be a bitter disappointment for me when compared to the friendly and tidy towns of Santa Barbara and San Diego. It was in the middle of a harsh desert, close to the Mexican border. Summer weather in this desert was unforgiving most every day, with temperatures often climbing into the 115 degree range. One big redeeming factor was its dry weather, very favorable for flying almost 365 days of the year.

Real air conditioning for the barracks buildings did not exist. Cooling was crudely implemented with the use of an ineffective makeshift system. Each two story barracks had a huge cube of hay, about four feet square, mounted over a wall opening that looked into the sleeping quarters. A large fan was mounted over the opposing side of the bale. Then a simple mechanism provided a constant dripping of water into the bale, with the fan simply providing a steady airstream through the wet hay and into the sleeping quarters. Only the bunks near the entering cool air stream felt appreciable relief. Ranking NCOs would be the typical occupants of this area. The rest of us would be dealt a paltry amount of relief from the heat.

All military bases are known to have post exchanges and also a slop shute. El Centro did have such a refuge, but unfortunately it was, for unknown reasons, closed for two or three weeks out of almost every month. Also, the chow served at the mess hall could only be described as pitiful. A rumor later abounded that the officers responsible for recreation and mess would later come under scrutiny and possible court martial for dereliction of duties. There really was no incentive to stay on the base on evenings or weekends. The alternate choice was for one to spend every opportunity in town. Air conditioning here was also scarce. The USO, the movies, and a few bars/motels were the exceptions. San Diego was too far away for an overnight liberty, as was also Los Angeles. Transportation to the town was provided with the use of what we called cattle cars, similar to those made for transporting cattle. They had open sides and no seats. Everybody stood. When densely crowded, room could always be made, with some effort, to accommodate (or pack in) one more body. To the east lay a vast expanse of desert reaching into Arizona, with its first large town of Tucson about 250 miles away. About 15 miles to the south on the border with Mexico, sat the bustling town of Calexico. On the Mexican side of the border sat the town of Mexicali. Neither of these towns appealed to me. Surrounding El Centro were only a few tiny towns worth visiting, maybe once or twice, like Brawley, Imperial, Heber and Seeley.

First Liberty in El Centro, early 1945
Charley Prester, Art Harris, and Kelly

I did become good pals with two other veteran Marines, Art Harris, a Kansas native, and Charlie Prester, from Hackensack, NJ. Both were a few years older than I. Charlie was committed to a girl back home. Art was married and had a toddler son. His little family lived in Sanford, FL. He spoke of them only on occasion. We all enjoyed the same common cause; stay true to our loved ones back home. The typical format for an evening's liberty in El Centro was for us to first check our jackets or military blouses at the USO. They would be needed for warmth upon returning to the base later at night in the open cattle cars provided for us. In town, we would usually start off by seeing a movie, followed by hitting a few bars. IDs were never checked in these desert towns. We would then hole up for the night in one of the town's few air conditioned motels. It was indeed a luxury to sleep the night in air conditioned comfort. Making out with girls while on liberty just never appeared on our agenda. In the morning we would top it off with a hearty, full breakfast and then return to camp.

26. BOMBARDIER SCHOOL

With many more veterans now returning from the war front, the authorities were facing a problem in finding new assignments for them. In early March of 1945, an enterprising young Marine Lieutenant, Tennessee native W.K. Buskirk, came up with a solution to the problem. He proposed starting up a Bombardier School at this airbase where its dry climate would allow for year-round flying conditions. The idea went over big with the brass. Those of us having graduated from Bombsight School while it was based in Virginia had already received aerial bombardier training, whereas the Bombsight School in Jacksonville included only simulated flight training. Our incoming students would all be recent graduates from Navigator School. There remained now the big problem of availability of proper equipment. Getting a supply of bombsights and related ground training equipment was not expected to be a problem, nor was the procurement of pilots and bombardier instructors.

The problem remaining was the availability of planes specifically designed for bombardier training. The Navy really had nothing to offer us. Lt. Buskirk then took to touring nearby US Air Corps bases, and at Vandenberg Air Corps Base he discovered a veritable treasure of available surplus bombardier equipment. He found it easy to get his hands on a half dozen Link ground training vehicles. The real prize, however, was in finding and leasing ten Air Corps AT-11 twin engine Beechcraft planes, built expressly for navigation and bombardier training. The Navy labeled these planes as

SNB-1. It took only a few weeks to get the planes flown to El Centro. Then in getting them flight worthy for regular duty, we discovered that acquiring the necessary spare parts might prove to be more difficult. Lt. Buskirk was quite the negotiator in this field, and occasionally used covert ways to get what he needed. Procuring equipment between different military branches could be challenging. We made a few trips back to Vandenberg where the Lt. would keep an Air Corps official distracted with conversation, while a few of his crew would actually sneak around the buildings and strip wanted parts off surplus planes parked in the area. We somehow got away with this thievery and were soon able to start operations at our new school in mid-March of 1945.

The training first started with a ground course and the use of Link trainer vehicles. (Remember that this portion of the course was thoroughly outlined in my previous discussion of bombardier training, in Virginia.) This phase simply got the student thoroughly familiar with the workings of the Bombsight, but proved not very exciting to an instructor. I had no trouble advancing to flight instructor, and made my first hop on March 17, 1945. The flight training course started with a marked-out 300 foot bullseye circle marked out on the desert floor as our stationary target. The plane flew at 8,000 feet, or a little below, such that there was no need for providing oxygen to the pilot, instructor or the three students on board. After a few fixed runs, hitting the target became a piece of cake, and catching the bullseye needed only a bit more practice.

The last two weeks of the course would prove much more challenging, since it involved hitting a target moving in a non-linear direction. This normally should not have presented a problem for the bombardier, since the bombsight automatically did correct for a target moving at a fixed speed in a linear direction. In this case, however, our twelve foot square target was mounted on top of a small armored vehicle which moved at a constant speed, but along the curved track of a 1,000 foot diameter circle. This track was to simulate the movement of an enemy warship under attack. The bombsight was unable to compute a correct flight path for a target moving in an arced direction. During the last few seconds of a bombing run, the bombardier had to make a single, overriding correction and put the plane on a slightly different intercept flight path. This involved a bit of guesswork, lots of practice, and a bit of luck.

Practice bombs were 30 lb. missiles, containing a smoke producing explosive charge, and did not present a danger to humans unless detonated very close by. Typical takeoff time was about 5:30 AM. The desert atmosphere was normally dry and typically free from rain squalls. By midday, land temperatures could soar to as much as 115 degrees, and generate very strong thermal air currents, making it just about impossible to hold the plane at a steady altitude. This condition usually caused it necessary to quit flying by 11 AM. Frequent airsickness during these rough flights became a real menace, especially for the students, since they were seated well toward the rear of the plane where the ride could be quite rocky.

One day, a bomber pilot from outside the school wanted to experience the feeling of what it was like to drop bombs by using the Bombsight. Unexpectedly, that day's unusually bad thermal air currents got to him, causing him to throw up all over the bombsight and adjacent equipment. After landing, he was made to clean up his mess. It never did happen to me, although I did come close a few times, as a result of the stench of being cooped up with students all suffering the tribulations of airsickness.

The SNB was a gorgeous twin-engine plane, and also considered a popular civilian transport. It used twin rudders, making turn and bank maneuvers very easy. The pilot's responsibility was simple: get to the target (about 15 minutes), and get back. The instructor and student took over the controls as the ground target was sighted. The bombsight was then employed to lock into the plane's autopilot and subsequently take over the bombing run all the way to the target. During each bombing run, the pilot had simply to keep the plane's airspeed and altitude very steady, ultimately turning his task into a very boring one.

Having a co-pilot aboard was not deemed a necessity. I was allowed to sit in that seat and occasionally fly the plane manually to the target area. Boy, this was real fun. In the beginning, the school's agenda started with one flight a day, each carrying three students. But after becoming enamored with this dream task, I insisted on, and occasionally was granted twice-daily flights. This practice ended abruptly one day when I developed ear problems and was temporarily grounded. I thoroughly enjoyed my role as a flight instructor, especially for having to meet the challenges of a target moving along a circular path. You could say that I was becoming addicted. I remember well the exhilaration experienced each morning while in the copilot's seat, as the plane raced down the runway and became airborne. To me, these flights were the thrill of a lifetime, and the highlight of my entire Marine Corps career.

Beechcraft SNB-1 Bombardier Trainer

Norden Bombsight and stabilizer gyro, as mounted in the plane's nose

Kelly, with three students, ready for a flight lesson, 1945

Now, how about our combat pilots? Would they call this R&R? Were they addicted like I was, or at least having fun? Hell no! Most were literally bored out of their skulls! As I would turn from the bombardier's station up front, and yell to the pilot: "We're done, let's go home"....the real action took place. Some pilots' reactions were rather pronounced. I flew with ten different pilots in the group, and maybe two or three would casually fly us back to the air base. As to the others, one had a passion for pushing the throttles wide-open, and then head straight for the landscape below, where we would drop out of the sky like a rock and then go zipping along the desert floor looking for anything that might serve as a target. Typical ones would be the winding storm gullies that cut across the desert. These were ditches, 50 to 100 feet wide, and about six feet deep, carved out by flood waters that occasionally raged through the desert. There also existed a vast grid of high tension wires that crossed the countryside. Also to be found were a few cattle ranches spread about. Those poor grazing cattle! They found little peace during these morning hours.

I loved every minute of it. Now, this is what you call R&R! It seems other pilots had their own way of getting their jollies. But the one that topped them all was that of flying along the straight highways which endlessly crossed the desert expanse and having no towns or buildings that might require caution by a low flying aircraft. Here was a rare opportunity for a hotshot pilot because he couldn't do this in a metropolitan area. With the throttle wide open and reaching 220 mph, he literally hugged the road, and I do mean the pavement itself, such that he would have to pick up a wing tip in order to clear each of the periodic five foot high road signs that were strung along both sides of the highway. Now, this is what you call living! However, during one of these larks, and with both of us concentrating on spotting the oncoming stationary road signs, a trailer truck suddenly loomed directly in our path. He had literally popped up out of one of those deep, desert gullies, being invisible to us until that last split second.

I will never forget the terrified look on that truck driver's face as we flashed by. The pilot instinctively yanked back on the stick and very narrowly avoided a collision with the truck. A moment before, we saw the terrified truck driver throwing his arms up and around his face, expecting the inevitable. Then as we ascended and banked to the left, we observed the truck in a cloud of dust, sailing off the highway and across the desert floor, but still upright and going straight. We sincerely hope this incident didn't leave the poor driver with a heart problem or with perpetual nightmares.

Other pilots got their thrills in different ways. Fighter pilots seemed to have a fixation on retracting the landing gear while the planes' wheels were still on the ground. The idea was to become airborne at the lowest possible minimum speed. Typically, retracting the landing gear gives the plane an instant 2-4 mph boost in air speed. A pilot should retract the landing gear only after he feels the plane becoming airborne. But most fighter pilots seem to feel differently about this. On takeoff, and sitting in the co-pilot's seat, I was often instructed to wait for his signal to have me reach over and flip the landing gear switch to the up position. The first time I did this routine, I was naïve, and was momentarily terrified as I felt the plane actually sink down for a second. We had not yet been airborne, not until the gear was retracted. But this is what a salty fighter pilot likes to do. Afterwards, I learned to take an extra second when about to reach over and flip that switch...

Another pilot also liked doing this maneuver, but this time while airborne, high up in the sky. He would crank back the throttles little by little, and when approaching the stall speed, he would casually lower the landing gear, further slowing down the plane. Very slowly he would then continue to ease back on the throttles while having me standing by with my finger over the wheels up switch. He would continue this nerve wracking practice until the plane started shaking and vibrating, a sure indication we were about to stall. At that point, even revving the engines might not pull us out of the stall. When he felt the point of no return had been reached, he gently pushed the stick forward and simultaneously had me flip the gear up switch, thus giving us that small boost in airspeed. He loved this! I hated flying with this guy. He was the only pilot to indulge in this dangerous practice. For thrills, I much preferred getting my jollies by taking part in high speed antics along the desert floor.

In April, I had the startling experience of running into Freddie Corbitt, a colleague from the old outfit in Santa Barbara that had shipped out without me. Freddie had just returned from carrier duty overseas and had a very sad story to tell. His squadron had been assigned to an aircraft carrier, the Franklin, as part of a naval task force in a new important venture of softening up airfields on the homeland island of Kyushu, Japan, and in preparation for the big invasion of Okinawa to take place some two weeks later. In the recent past, some raids had been delivered on a hit and run basis. Now, these carriers would remain in the area and ultimately take part in the invasion of Okinawa. Up to mid-1944, Marine Aviation had only participated in a few operations from aircraft carriers. Now, they would be involved in a major carrier offensive off the coast of homeland Japan. Santa Barbara had been the center for the training of Marine Air Groups operating off aircraft carriers. Our men from MAG 42 who recently shipped out from Santa Barbara were to be pioneers in this bold venture.

On March 19, 1945, aboard the Franklin, Freddie's squadron along with another, had just finished launching about 2/3 of its combat planes when a Kamikaze plane suddenly dropped out of the clouds 2,000 feet above, and scored direct hits with two 500 lb. bombs. On deck and ready to launch, were five dive bombers, fourteen torpedo planes, and twelve fighter planes, all laden with fuel and bombs. Most of the bombs on these waiting aircraft were set off by the falling Japanese bombs, creating an inferno as never before seen in Pacific carrier warfare. Shortly after, tremendous explosions took place on the flight deck and the hangar decks below.

In June of 2014, I happened to share the company of a salty old Marine, Bob Denton, a veteran who served as a Marine gunner aboard the light Navy cruiser, the USS Cabot. His ship was one of several which were quick to come to the aid of the burning Franklin. The scene of the several ships frantically trying to rescue the many sailors abandoning ship was that of bedlam. The Franklin presented a terrifying sight to the rest of Naval Task Force 58. The Cabot also helped in fighting the fires that freely raged aboard the stricken carrier. Bob Denton had a hard time in describing the immensity of this disaster, only saying that it was "Bad... REALLY bad." In all, from the two Marine fighter plane squadrons, there were 65 aviation personnel killed, comprised of seven officers and 58 enlisted men. These two squadrons were out of action after only two days of carrier combat.

Freddie was in real bad shape psychologically. He had a hard time relating the grizzly events of that fateful day. He did dwell on one event in particular, which described the conditions of the area below decks, where some of his buddies had not survived. These men were found trapped in a sealed-off compartment in the hangar deck below, all huddled in different body positions. All were burned to death, essentially cremated. I later accompanied Freddie on a liberty in San Diego, where he looked for ways to ease his anxieties. We spent the afternoon at the popular amusement park at Mission Beach. Freddie wanted only to ride the park's famous roller coaster, over and over again. Afterwards, I met his mother, who had come out west to live with him. She was heartbroken in finding him so disturbed. I do believe he eventually did get hospitalized and hopefully treated for PTSD.

My first official flight as an instructor took place on March 17, 1945. Soon after that, I got word from back home that my older brother Henry, who had just finished 32 bombing missions as a tail gunner aboard B-24s and B-17s over Europe and Germany, had recently returned to the States, and was now assigned to a huge Air Corps base outside of Tucson, AZ, a distance of only 300 miles from El Centro. He was stationed there for training as a gunner on the new Superfortress, the B-29, in preparation for the planned, oncoming long range bombing of cities on the Japanese mainland.

I hadn't seen, nor heard from Henry in more than two years, and I thought, boy...wouldn't it be great to pay him a surprise visit? We should have lots to talk about, considering both having just returned from overseas duty. The question was: How do I get there, and do I make the journey alone? This was still war time with its strict gasoline rationing and sparse highway traffic. Fortunately, I was able talk my good liberty pal, Art Harris, into making this adventurous trip with me. He was several years older than I, and a lot wiser. With him at my side, I felt certain we could pull it off and have a great time. For transportation, we had the choice of grabbing a bus which ran on a lean schedule between San Diego and Texas, or to rough it by hitch hiking our way to Tucson.

On May 06, 1945, we set out to hitch hike the first leg of our journey, about 60 miles. This took us along a single highway through some of the bleakest parts of the desert leading to the border with Arizona. After what seemed like hours of standing on the edge of the highway, we were finally rewarded with a ride aboard an open bed truck. Hesitantly, we climbed aboard. When sitting with your back to the airflow, the sun literally barbecued you. But if you stood up and faced the airflow, it felt like a blowtorch in your face. We reluctantly chose the former.

Somehow surviving the ride across the open desert, we finally crossed the border, and approached the small town of Yuma, Arizona. Here was a fork in the road and our driver was heading north. After disembarking at the intersection, we were shocked to find a dozen or so uniformed Army soldiers scattered about the intersection, and just like us, obviously looking for a lift to somewhere. There must have been an Army base nearby. At this point, the situation looked somewhat hopeless, so we tentatively decided to chuck the whole idea of a trip to Tucson and instead catch a bus back to El Centro. First, we decided to drop in a diner at the intersection, and have some refreshments. There, we were further saddened upon noting more soldiers seated inside, undoubtedly also waiting for a ride. There were also a few civilians, one of whom sat right next to me. He was accompanied by a young boy, probably his son or nephew. After a few moments of silence, and without turning his face to me, the man asked where we were headed, to which I replied... "Tucson". Another moment of silence... Then he said "I'm goin' right by there, I'll take ya." Boy did that get our attention! No need to turn back now. Art and I would be comfortably seated in a closed vehicle. As we filed out of the diner, we had to pass through the group of soldiers standing about. They didn't look happy on seeing these two Marines steal this ride from right under their noses. While making our way to our civilian's car, we kept our eyes trained straight ahead, thus avoiding the soldiers' icy glares.

After several hours comfortably seated inside this Texas-bound vehicle, and with very little conversation, the driver made his way into the city of Tucson. I had already told him the reason for our trip, and now added we would first like to look for tonight's lodging. Without comment, he changed directions and dropped us off at a rather swanky hotel. Inside, as Art and I approached the hotel counter, we noted quite a few Army personnel milling about, mostly officers, and were then shocked at hearing the desk clerk explaining to a rather disappointed Army officer, that there were no rooms available here for the night, and to his knowledge, at any other hotel in town. Once again, Art and I got mentally prepared to turn right around and take that bus back to El Centro. As the Army officer turned to leave, we were surprised to hear the desk clerk address us with: "Anything I can do for you Marines?" A little flabbergasted with this courteous greeting, I quietly proceeded to tell the clerk of our long journey over the desert in hopes of seeing my Air Corps brother who was stationed just outside of town. Without a word, the clerk started thumbing through his ledger, and then cheerfully announced that he could set us up in the hotel's one and only bridal suite! We were delighted! Boy, this Marine uniform sure does get results.

Now brimming with our recent good luck experiences, we headed for Henry's sprawling military base. All we had was his Air Corps mailing address. After getting to the base's guardhouse with little trouble, we were courteously directed to Henry's squadron headquarters and finally ushered into the office of the air base Adjutant, a stern-looking, comfortably seated Major. After being told the reason for our visit, the Major became a little agitated, then hemmed and hawed about any prospects of our being allowed to see Henry, or of allowing him freedom to go on liberty with us.

Finally, it came out... Henry was on barracks detention, a mild form of court martial. We were told that in a recent incident, Henry, for some reason, had taken a poke at a Lieutenant. Henry obviously was unhappy with his new assignment so soon after the ordeals of his many bombing missions over Nazi-occupied Europe. The Major was adamant. Henry had to be punished for his deed, and to give him off-base liberty would be out of the question. It was here-we-go-again time for Art and me.

Brother, Henry Augustyniak – Sgt, US Air Corps, circa 1944

For sure, this time we would have to admit defeat, abort the mission and head back to El Centro. However, having made it so far in this journey, I suddenly became inspired to launch an all-out nonstop emotional plea, relating that I hadn't seen my brother for three years, that Henry had just returned after serving 32 bombing missions over Europe, and that I had just returned from an 18 month tour of duty in the South Pacific. And further adding that Art and I had experienced great difficulties in getting this far into our journey, and that it would be a huge disappointment for us to have to return without seeing Henry. At this point, I was merely hoping for a brief visit with Henry in his barracks.

The Major, obviously troubled with having to make a heartless decision on Henry's confinement, hemmed and hawed some more, then grumbling, made this startling announcement: "Alright, alright, he can have a three day liberty pass with you, but he'll still have to make up for his bad behavior at a later time." WOW!... we were almost floored to hear this incredible news. This Marine uniform came through again, this time with flying colors!!

When we found Henry, he was sitting woefully on the edge of his bunk. His despair quickly turned to delight as he set eyes on his "baby" brother with his Marine friend. Then when told of the three day pass, he became ecstatic. This turn of events was hard to believe. Three days of liberty in town with family and friends sure trumps sitting on your bunk to await disciplinary action. Our hotel bridal suite accommodation turned out to be one of true luxury, one which few ordinary servicemen would ever experience. For three days and nights, the three of us lapped up the luxury and had a grand time just doing the town. Two brothers were experiencing the rare occasion of getting together in this remote region of the USA and trading all their recent wartime experiences. Hating to see it end, we reluctantly bid a quick goodbye to Henry. Our subsequent bus ride back to El Centro wasn't that bad after all, since Art and I were able to bask in the fond memories of this adventurous trip across this vast, desolate desert region of the USA.

In early July, 1945, with the Pacific war now appreciably winding down, a decision was made to close down our flight school. Bombardiers were now becoming somewhat superfluous. However, as an instructor, I felt I had one particular piece of unfinished business to attend to. The frustration of never having hit that moving target drove me to dream up a wild scheme. Remember that the target was a twelve foot square wooden frame that held painted diagonal black and white stripes, and was mounted on the roof of a small armored vehicle. During the bombing runs this vehicle sped around a fixed circle of about 1,000 foot diameter. Its drivers were a couple of sailors, stationed nearby expressly for this purpose.

Since the vehicle was in a constant turn, it was almost impossible to hit. Our turning target simulated a warship in the defensive move of tacking, as in a tight turn. This principle was vividly portrayed in some TV wartime documentaries showing an actual warship in a tight turn while under air attack, leaving a characteristic wake behind, and then have an aerial bomb explode dead ahead of the exact spot the ship would have been had it kept on a straight course. Special training aimed at overcoming the Bombsight's deficiency was the last phase on the student's course. In the four months of five days per week bombing runs, each with three students, no one had ever been lucky enough to score a direct hit on this small moving target. However, the relative size of the targets did have a big bearing on the success of scoring a direct hit, since our twelve foot square desert target was about 40 times smaller than that of an average warship.

This special course taught the implementation of a deliberate manual correction to change the plane's flight path to one slightly parallel to the one calculated by the bombsight. Otherwise, the bombsight had full control of the plane's flight course. The deliberate correction was judiciously done only a few seconds before each bomb was about to be automatically released by the bombsight. The student had to choose the exact moment to have the plane shifted over to a parallel course that would then have the released bomb intercept the target on its curved path. To determine the exact moment of correction, the bombardier had to frequently pull away from the telescope to observe the position of two moving indices (markers) on the bombsight that were moving toward each other. When they met, the bomb would automatically be released. The student would only have 5-10 seconds before the bomb's automatic release to make the appropriate course correction. If he made the correction too close to the time of the bomb's release, the bomb would be ejected while in the process of banking, thus flipping it out laterally. We had a few occasions where, under these conditions, the bomb landed almost a mile from its target. This maneuver was extremely tricky and had to be much practiced before any degree of success could be achieved.

In our daily runs, bombs were released one at a time. In my new wild scheme, all eight bombs would be dropped simultaneously. The students were instructed to remove all eight bombs from the bomb bay racks and line them up loosely on the walkway between the parallel bomb bays. At the exact moment the indicators showed the bomb about to be automatically released, all the bombs would be simultaneously shoved, or kicked out. Being the very last day of school, I had no problem in talking that day's pilot into going along with my scheme. Most of the pilots were game for any wild idea, since their boring jobs could always use a little excitement. I personally handled the bombsight during that run, and at my signal, the students simultaneously shoved all the bombs off the walkway and into the open bomb bays. The pilot then immediately took over the controls, banking the plane into an arced path to see how we did.

What we witnessed was somewhat unnerving. There no longer was any sign of the armored vehicle, only a huge cloud of smoke! We surely did hit the target this time. We then proceeded to circle around, looking for any movement around the scene. When the smoke cleared, it showed a stationary vehicle with the attached and demolished target dangling off its mount. Being a little concerned about this unexpected turn of events, the pilot then took us in for a closer look, buzzing the vehicle. Still no sign of life! We spent many minutes flying around, and finally, with much apprehension, had to give up and head for home. As we approached the airbase, we received a radio message with stern orders to report to headquarters immediately upon landing. We were in for it!

Later, as we sheepishly stood at attention in front of our stern Commanding Officer, he demanded: "What in Hell were you goofballs trying to do up there, kill those poor swabbies?" It turned out that most of the bombs had landed directly on the target, knocking out the vehicle's engine, and scaring the sailors half out of their wits. They were then afraid to come out. And when we swooped in for a closer look, they thought those crazy Gyrenes (a name sailors call Marines) were coming in to finish them off! They dared not venture out of the safe haven of their armored vehicle, and waited patiently until our plane disappeared. Amazingly, we received no punishment for this bad antic, only a reprimand, but had there been Marines instead of sailors inside that vehicle, the book may have been thrown at us. Like what we previously had done to the poor truck driver on that desert highway, this stunt would not be included on the recommended list as R&R for Marine pilots or future bombardiers.

The Last Flight - Bombs Away

Two days later, on July 09, 1945, we conducted our final flight as a five plane formation bombing run over the stationery 300 foot circle target. The pilot leading the formation was Lt. Buskirk, the head of our school. The lead bombardier was our senior NCO, Sgt. Alexander, whose bombsight would determine the exact course and time for the formation of planes to drop their string of bombs. Alex was known to like his booze. That morning, as a result of his night-before overindulgence, the bombs barely grazed the 300 foot circular target. Oh well, school was over, and we were just having a little fun.

27. LIVING IT UP

A few days later, Lt. Buskirk decided we should extend this fun time a bit more by having a group picnic. Since there was no hospitable area for an outing in the entire Imperial Valley desert, a State park in the adjacent Laguna Mountains, situated between San Diego and El Centro, was chosen. Laguna Park sat at an elevation of 6,000 feet, quite a contrast to the hot, dry valley below. Several open bed trucks were obtained and loaded with food of all sorts, and many cases of beer. The participants numbered about 25. My good friends Art Harris, Charlie Prester, and Pete Gathings were aboard. Pete was married to Jenny, a Navy WAVE (Women's Reserve) stationed in San

Diego, who was able to conveniently hop a bus from her base and meet us at the Park. The bus route ran east-west, right through the Park. The Park contained a few simple rides to have fun on, but the most enjoyment came from eating and drinking. I felt in a particularly good mood, and was later claimed by my peers to have guzzled a dozen bottles of beer and downed a dozen hard boiled eggs.

This claim may have been only slightly exaggerated because afterwards, I pulled off a rather foolish stunt. As the party was winding down and it was time for Jenny to catch the east bound bus back to San Diego, the five of us hiked over to the highway to intercept the bus. This was not a scheduled bus stop, so you had to hail it along the open highway. There was some concern that the bus, traveling at a high rate of speed, might fail to slow down or stop. However, with my courage pumped up as a result of consuming all that brew, I assured everyone that I would get the bus to stop for Jenny. And so, as it came barreling down the highway, I simply wandered out in the middle of the road and sat down. Fortunately, there were no other vehicles coming in either direction. The bus driver took instant note of the crazy serviceman and was able to stop in plenty of time. However, he was rather upset with this wild antic and expressed a strong desire to report me to the proper authorities. The scene ended without further incident, and Jenny got aboard, making the trip back to duty at her base at San Diego.

The rest of the party stayed until almost dark, then we packed all our gear and headed back to the sweltering desert barracks. With all that beer sloshing around inside me, I made the choice to ride in the open truck bed, rather than in the cab. I harbored fears of possibly needing to empty my bladder, or my stomach along the route back, but wanted to avoid causing any emergency stops. The one thing I didn't take into account was the mountain's chilly temperatures. The truck was not completely empty when we acquired it, but contained a pile of regular GI bunk bed mattresses on its cargo floor. To avoid freezing, I got real cozy by simply crawling between a few layers of them and it wasn't long before I fell sound asleep. The truck did make one pit stop for the crew in the cab, who became somewhat alarmed when they walked around back to check on me, but saw no sign of life in the back of the truck. I could have fallen off the truck, but they reasoned that it was more likely that I switched trucks at the last minute. Upon arrival at the air base, and accounting for all bodies, everyone breathed a sense of relief.

With the school having been shut down, instructors were immediately assigned a new ordnance duty, that of modifying brand new twin engine fighter planes by Grumman, the F7F Tigercat. These were the Navy's first twin engine fighter planes. However, they proved to be too large for the existing Navy aircraft carriers ships, and so they were handed over to the Marines to be used in land based operations. We got real busy installing the necessary hardware for these planes to carry and dispense rocket-propelled bombs. Life at the base took on a more relaxed atmosphere with the war effort looking so much more in our favor. I found myself getting more involved in going on liberty just about every evening and seriously taking up drinking the hard stuff. How this change came about was hard to understand. I may have been dwelling too much on Freddie's sordid story of my Santa Barbara buddies' terrible fate and the distinct possibility that had I stayed with the outfit when they shipped out of Santa Barbara, that I wouldn't be alive today.

Art and I had become great liberty buddies while serving as instructors, but even more so, by spending many drinking liberties together. I now found it easy to down hard liquor. We no longer spent pleasant overnights in town, and we had lost Charlie as a liberty pal, as he had been reassigned. It was now just Art and me. We soon started visiting dinky bars in the surrounding little towns of Brawley, Holtville and Heber. Art picked up an old used car, so visiting these remote towns was not a problem. One day we somehow came across an unattended, unopened case of Old Crow bourbon whiskey. Name brand alcoholic beverages were very scarce during the war years. We worked on this liquid treasure almost daily, although never putting a finish to it. Perhaps I had finally entered the coming of age period, or just plain grew up. Boozing now seemed to be a regular part of my new life.

Then one day, Art came across with some jolting news for me. His wife Irene, their infant son, and Irene's mother were coming to live with him off base. I had only vaguely been aware that he was married, since he seldom talked about his marriage or having a family. Our boozing days were now over. I tried teaming up with a new individual, named Raul. He happened to be very fond of the rum drink called Cuba Libra, which I found rather unappealing. On our first liberty together, I got somewhat cocky and boasted that I could down a shot of every bottle of liquor currently displayed on the back wall of the bar. He challenged me to do it, which I did, and much to his chagrin, remained cold sober. Raul was impressed, but in a negative way. Afterwards, he no longer sought my companionship.

Afterwards, I was unable to find another drinking partner. Somehow, the allure of solitary boozing on hard liquor had finally lost all its allure, and I returned to being a simple 20 year old kid who liked to hoist a few beers in the local slop shutes, and go about with the simple military life.

Life was good now. On September 22, 1945, I turned 21 years old. I had an old score to settle with all those upscale bars in San Diego that had previously refused to serve me any alcohol because of my age. There would no longer be any humiliation for this veteran Marine when visiting a bar in the big city. I made a distinct special liberty to town and proceeded to regale in the experience of entering many bars that day and to deliberately flash my ID card up real close in the face of ID checkers, verifying that I indeed was 21.

Satisfaction….. finally!

28. HEADING HOME

The war in the Pacific had been turning in our favor for some time now, but was still expected to last for several more years, probably producing catastrophic casualties. However, following the atomic bombings of Hiroshima and Nagasaki on August 6 and 9 of 1945, it all came to a rather abrupt end, with Japan officially surrendering on August 14, 1945. Life should be good now, right? But, as a civilian, what would the future hold for a 21 year old, who had never held a solid job in his youthful lifetime? Maybe I should ship over, that is to sign up for another four years in the military and let Uncle Sam take care of my everyday needs. My first tour of duty had just ended on my birthday, September 22. All our military organizations were now swamped with processing servicemen being mustered out as fast as they could. However, I was held to my duties under a government program called "Held at the Convenience of the Government," and flabbergasted after receiving recurring calls from the front office, asking me to consider shipping over. I just didn't feel that I possessed any special skills that made me needed. When I wrote to my sweetheart back home that I was considering shipping over for another four years, her answer was emphatic and unambiguous..."NO WAY!" Anyway, I would have been out of my mind to consider doing any additional duty while stationed at this miserable military airbase.

In early November, 1945, I was called in for a final meeting by my superiors and told my discharge papers were all in order and I was scheduled to leave on, or after November 3rd. The plan was to travel by train to the vast US Navy Training Center in Bainbridge, MD for final discharge from the Corps. When I conveyed this good news to my sweetheart, she replied cheerfully with news that her first cousin, Calvin Pezzner, was stationed there and held the high rank as the base's chief cook and mess officer. Shortly after arriving at the processing base in Maryland, I found Calvin roaming around in a vast dining hall, one capable of seating and feeding many hundred servicemen at a time. After cordial greetings, he asked: "Walt, when's the last time you had a good steak?" I promptly replied that it was so long ago that I couldn't remember. "Sit down here," he said, and proceeded to call over a Navy cook and a few attendants to the table. "Tell them exactly what you want and how you'd like it." The time was about 10:30 AM in the morning, and the hall was completely empty of other patrons. I felt kind of out of place, but he assured me that I would be well taken care of. Needless to say, I proceeded to have the biggest, most delicious steak I ever had, or would ever have, all with compliments of Calvin and the US Navy. He stayed with me long enough to see that I received the treatment of a dignitary.

A week later, a simple discharge ceremony followed, and I was sent on my way back home to Ashley, PA, as a civilian. My final homecoming that day was truly a happy one for me, my concerned parents, and especially for my sweetheart, Neshie. We both were now very anxious to start a new life together as adults, and no longer as puppy-lovesick teenagers.

The date is November 11, 1945.

WELCOME TO A BRAND-NEW WORLD.

EPILOGUE

KEEPING IN TOUCH WITH OLD COMRADES

Henry Simek

I had several phone talks with Henry over the years. The last one told of having eight children at that time, and that they were always full of chatter all the time, a real joy in his life.

On December 07, 1987, I received an informative letter from his wife, Peg that told they had raised a total of 12 children together! Henry retired from two full-time jobs two years ago. Now they liked traveling to Kripplebush, NY, near Kingston, where Peg's parents lived. Henry thought about stopping by my Bridgewater, NJ home for a visit, but my winter stays in Florida nixed that. Peg mentioned seeing Ray Cope who was in our outfit in Samoa. One day, while attending school in New York City some years after getting out of the service, I ran into Ray on Columbus Circle.

On December 20, 1992, I wrote a long letter to Henry and Peg, telling of my life since discharge. A Christmas card from Peg in 1998 told of Henry's passing away on November 20, 1998, as a result of cardio/lung problems.

A following Christmas card in 1999 from Peg detailed how Henry was a stay-at-home guy after retirement, seemingly all burned out from having worked two jobs in support of his large family. He had been sick for 3½ years, not wanting to leave the house. They had 53½ years together. She mentioned Ray Cope again. Ray had married Peg's good friend, but then died about five years ago.

A Christmas card in 2000 from Henry and Peg's family told of Peg's passing away on September 22, 2000 from cancer.

Leon Augustyn

On April 20, 1986, after my sending their family a long letter describing my association and adventures with Leon in Samoa, his son Ronald responded and told that he was aware that Leon and I had exchanged Christmas cards every year. He told that Leon did not marry his childhood sweetheart, Evelyn, as he had fondly talked of doing while in Samoa. Afterwards, he had been stationed in DC where he met his future wife, Mary. They had two children, Ronald and Ellen. They then moved back to Chicago and he resumed his pre-war job as a tool and die maker for the Goodman Company.

Leon and Mary separated after 18 years of marriage. He remarried, but divorced again after a short time, and wound up moving in with Ronald and his wife. Ronald enjoyed these years and remained very close with his Dad. Leon's first wife, Mary, remained a close friend to the family throughout the years. Leon retired at age 62. On November 19, 1985, he died of a heart attack.

Wilfred Gagnon

On August 24, 1946, responding to a letter received from me, "Willie" recounted having run into a few Marines we had served with together. One was Dewitt Mosby, who was from Memphis and with whom I had served in San Diego just before shipping overseas. After Bombsight School, Willie was stationed in Cherry Point, NC and Quantico, while working on Norden Bombsights. He entered flight school in January of 1944, and attended schools in Louisiana, Texas, Georgia and Tennessee, where he eventually gave up the pursuit of becoming a pilot. He then shipped overseas to Okinawa in June of 1945, then to Yokohama, Japan, came back in January of 1946, and was discharged in February.

After a short stay at home in Maine, he moved to Buffalo, NY, hoping to attend college there. Unable to get accepted locally, he then applied to and was accepted by the University of Toronto, in Canada. He succeeded in earning a degree, and eventually enjoyed a successful career in Psychology.

He had not married his childhood sweetheart, Muriel. He finished his letter by philosophizing a bit about how, during our friendship in Quantico and Dahlgren, I had constantly worried that things would not work out for me later in life. At that time I had predicted that Willie might make a good psychologist. Seems I may have been right.

Art Harris

His August 28, 1946 letter told of him no longer working for the railroad, because of having spent too much time away from home. He switched jobs and now worked as and liked being a carpenter. With a GI loan, he and Irene had bought a nice home just outside of Sanford, FL. Son, Donnie was just learning to speak whole words. He invited me to come down to Florida after I married Neshie, and said we should spend our honeymoon with them. He even said I should settle down in Florida after getting married and finishing aircraft instrument school.

A few years later in speaking with him via telephone I was to learn that his wife and two children had suffered a heart wrenching tragedy. While he was away on the job, his home burned down with the family inside, with everyone suffering severe burns. One child didn't survive and the other had to spend many weeks in the hospital. The family then moved away, after which I lost contact with him.

Colonel Benjamin Reisweber

A few years ago, I was able to reach members of Ben's family and learn of his early years, and also where he served after leaving Samoa in mid-1945. He was born in 1894. When WWI came along, he joined the Marine Corps and trained as a pilot. The war ended as he was boarding ship for duty in the Europe. He then left the active service and worked as a private pilot for a business executive, during which time he suffered a serious accident and was told he would never walk again. He proved everyone wrong, recovered, and returned to active military duty, but never allowed to pilot a plane again. In the early 1930s, he was a captain and commanding officer of a Marine Air Detachment in NY. At the outbreak of WWII, he served as commanding officer of a training squadron in Pensacola, FL.

In 1942, the Colonel reported for duty in San Diego, where he assumed command of MCAF headed for special duty in the South Pacific. After returning in1945, he shipped out to the island of Peleliu, on the Palau island chain, where he assumed duties as a Wings Operation Officer of a Marine Air Wing. Rumor had it that despite being grounded, he managed to take a fighter plane up for a ride while on duty in the Pacific,… just for the love of flying.

After the war, he returned to duty in the DC area, retired in 1950, and died in 1969. He is now interred fittingly in Arlington National Cemetery.

ITINERARY

DUTY WITH THE MARINES

Sept 23, 1941 .... Boot Camp, Parris Island, SC

Nov 28, 1941 .... MCAS, Quantico, VA

Apr 30, 1942 .... Naval Proving Grounds, Dahlgren, VA

Aug 08, 1942 .... NAS, San Diego, CA

Dec 15, 1942 - May 16, 1944 .... MCAF, Tutuila, Samoa

Jun - Aug 1944 .... Camp Miramar, San Diego, CA

Sept 02, 1944 .... MCAS, Santa Barbara, CA

Jan 27, 1945 .... MCAS, El Centro, CA

Nov 11, 1945 .... Discharged, at Bainbridge, MD

POST-WAR ACTIVITIES

Walt moved from Wilkes Barre, PA, to New York City in early 1946. He was briefly employed by Con Edison, and then attended The School for Aircraft Instruments, in NYC for six months. On September 14, 1946, he married his childhood sweetheart, Gertrude "Neshie" Pezzner. After graduation, he found immediate employment as an instrument technician, with Lockheed Aircraft Services at MacArthur (Islip) and Idlewild (JFK) airports on Long Island, NY. He then brought Neshie out to start married life together in a little apartment in the town of Sayville, NY. Their first child, Nancy, came along on October 3, 1949.

In 1951, Walt took employment at Brookhaven National Labs on Long Island, where he spent two years working in the Nuclear Physics field. Their first son, Paul was born on April 15, 1953. Shortly after, he and the family moved to Morristown, NJ where he started work at Bell Telephone Labs, spending 33 years working in the field of Radiation Physics. On February 10, 1958, Michael was born. In 1961, the family moved to Bridgewater, NJ, where they remained for 29 years. After retiring in 1987, Walt worked as an atomic particle accelerator consultant to Harvard University for four years. After a five year hiatus, he returned to consulting to work for Vanderbilt University, serving eleven more years, and finally retiring for good in 2007.

After raising three children together and 66 years of wedded bliss, Neshie passed away on April 5, 2013. Walt currently resides in Barnegat, NJ, and enjoys keeping active, writing, fishing, and tinkering with WWII model planes.